NAVI

SUCCESSFUL

LIFE JOURNEY

A GUIDE TO PERSONAL AND FAMILY PROBLEM SOLVING

◊

DR. MARVIN A. JOHNSON

ISBN-13: 978-1546310501
ISBN-10: 1546310509

Acknowledgements and Thanks

This book was long in thinking, talking and planning but short in taking action. It has been discussed with friends and co-workers for years and it even had a couple of brief starts that faded away. The final push to really get going was done by a fellow member of my church, Mike Lauesen, who one Sunday said to me, "Stop talking about that book and JUST WRITE IT!" That final push did it, and the writing began for real! Thank you, Mike!

Also thanks to the hundreds of co-workers over the years who have been good examples and helped me learn and grow. Special thanks to the thousands of individuals, couples and families who have trusted me with their innermost feelings and desires. Sometimes you had to wait days for an appointment, plus you had to pay for it! I so appreciate all of you giving me a chance to be of help to you and trusting me with your secrets and deepest feelings, thoughts, and emotions.

Thanks to my wife, Mary Ellen, who was able to read my scribbled pages and type them into drafts and then to final chapters. As a Licensed Clinical Social Worker, she served as my consultant, provider of ideas and my listening ear. Beyond that, she was my active cheerleader and always supportive of my effort.

Also thanks to my sister, Ida, who edited and organized the material and arranged for the process of printing and presentation.

Over the years, I developed personal friendships with many of the professionals with whom I have worked. Many have suggested and supported my writing a book and tried to motivate me to do it. I worked a lot with Dr. Leo Jacobs, Psychiatrist, who was very supportive about my writing, and even after I retired, when our paths would cross, he would ask, "How is the book coming?" He was pleased to write his thoughts for this book's Foreword.

I owe thanks to many persons, including immediate and extended family for their ongoing support over the years. I have received thanks from thousands of patients with whom I have worked. Most are verbal thanks, maybe a brief note, or in some way letting me know our time together had been helpful. I am including three examples of special thanks for which I was touched, grateful and humbled.

A couple came in for therapy for several reasons, including his cancer diagnosis, which was an obvious threat to them. I worked with them for about two years, and after various treatments and multiple efforts by medical persons, he said in a session, "I think I am going to go south." This was his way of accepting dying, which he did a few days later. His wife continued therapy for a while after his death, and shortly before her last session, she brought in a Prayer Blanket that she and her children had made. Its edges had numerous knots, and she explained each knot was done with a prayer. Some were for me and for my work but also for others who are ill, persons needing help, medical personnel and others. She also emphasized that the family had actually done the individual prayers identified by the knots. I was very touched and always will treasure that quilt.

A single older lady came in for therapy and was actually seen off and on for several years. When she heard I was retiring, she wrote the letter below, thanking me and giving me the gift of a Bible, which I will keep forever:

I'm sitting here thinking about tomorrow being the last day we will be together as Dr. and patient, although I have also considered you a good friend. It is bitter sweet for me, as I'm sure it is for you leaving your life's vocation and entering a new chapter in your life. It is important to me that you know how much you have done for me and have meant to me all of these years. You have been a steadfast in my life... someone that I could trust and tell all of my most private secrets to, knowing that you wouldn't judge me or make me feel foolish or stupid. You gave me practical advice that I could apply to improve my life. I've learned tons from you and I can never thank you enough for that.

I wanted to give you a good-bye gift that would be from my heart. I couldn't think of one thing I thought worthy enough to give you that would express my feelings. I finally realized that I could give you the best gift of all and truly from my heart. That is giving you a Bible and in that way sharing with you my love and faith.

Thank you for teaching me so many different things. I would appreciate it if occasionally you would send me an email letting me know how you are getting along. I know that it is out of the norm so I will leave it up to you to do as you see fit. I was glad to hear that you have already started on your activities for after "working life." I think it is admirable that you will be helping others and keeping yourself busy. I think it says a lot for your character, but I always knew that you were a good person. That is why I learned to trust you so easily. I wish you only the best for you and your family.

The third example was a lady with ovarian cancer who I saw while volunteering for the Cancer Care Foundation. The following is her complete letter to the Foundation:

I am writing to thank you for providing me with someone to talk to when I was diagnosed with ovarian canter. Dr. Marvin Johnson came to my home many times when I was unable to leave my home due to my illness. Dr. Johnson was wonderful, caring and always encouraging.

It w ɜ so helpful to me, especially because it did not cost my anything. When you are ill, money is the last thing you can or need to think about. And when I was too sick to go out, someone came to me to help me with what I was going through.

I am now able to get out and have returned to work. I needed to start chemotherapy treatments but am able to continue working. I hope I won't need your services again, but knowing that you're there in case I need help, is wonderful.

Again, thank you for the wonderful service you provide to people when they need it the most. I want you to know that Dr. Johnson served a major part in my being able to return to what I now call a "normal" life. He's a great person and people like him make people who don't know what to do or how to handle it when they are told they have cancer, understand that what they're feeling is 'normal" and that there are ways to deal with their fears. Thanks for the wonderful service you provide.

And now my final note to all of you...
Thank you for choosing to read my book. I hope that it will be helpful in giving you more information or in providing guidance and assistance with the problems you may face. We all have to deal with challenges, but the goal is to keep trying and never give up.

Table of Contents

Foreword

During my career I have had the pleasure of knowing and working with hundreds of professionals who have devoted their lives to helping others. Together we have shared problem situations, consulted with one another, and been supportive of each other in times of need or crisis. Of course we also laughed together and shared some times of needed humor.

I asked three professionals, who have been important persons in my life, if they would write a brief foreword for the book. Thankfully they were more than willing. All are still working full time and don't yet have the fun of "Retirement," which I am now able to do. Their remarks are as follows:

———

Rev. Dr. Chuck Mize, Senior Pastor
Glenview Community Church, Glenview, IL

As you explore the wisdom in the pages of this book, you will soon discover that it is a tool for the realities of living; an anchor of perspective that centers us in the storms of mental, emotional and relational challenges and a guide for healthy and

———

whole living through and beyond the wounds that we all suffer.

Dr. Marvin Johnson is uncommonly gifted in his discipline. Having served for decades as a mental health professional, whose therapeutic conversations dug deep into countless lives, the expansive experience of his practice expands sterile theory with understandable real-world vignettes. The son of a farmer and Lutheran lay-pastor, who was raised in the sometimes severe realities of rural South Dakota life, Dr. Johnson's devout faith reminds us that we are primarily spiritual beings who live and move in love. Turn the page, and let this treasure of wisdom and perspective unfold!

――――

Dr. Leo Jacobs, Psychiatrist
Barrington Neuropsychiatric Medicine,
Barrington, IL

I have known Dr. Marvin Johnson for many years, as a friend and a fellow mental health professional. He has extensive administrative and clinical experience as well as has been participating in educational programs regarding mental health for the community.

As a therapist, he has earned the respect of many clinicians who have referred patients to him with outstanding results. He also knows when to ask for psychiatric consultation in dealing with patients with severe mental illness.

He has been very effective in treating patients with depression, anxiety, substance abuse and marital problems. He has brought more constructive meanings and purposes in their lives as well as resilience and assertive abilities in coping with stress.

———

Dr. Cheryl Borst, Psychologist,
Barrington Center for Counseling and
Psychotherapy, Barrington, IL

I have had the pleasure and privilege of knowing Dr. Marvin Johnson as a personal friend and professional colleague for over 25 years. He has a wealth of experience from his years as the Director of the Social Work Department at a large Metropolitan Hospital, as past President of the Illinois Chapter of the National Association of Social Work, and Chairman of the Illinois Association for Marital and Family Therapists. He was a clinician in our large group practice and finally, with his pro-bono work with cancer patients and in Hospice.

———

I feel qualified and honored to endorse this book. I have spent many hours over the years watching his coaching techniques applied in actual sessions and know they work. As a mentor, Marvin has taught me compassion, integrity, practicality and professionalism. In this book, he doesn't just give you conclusions. Like a trusted friend, he provides recommendations, suggestions and information to help you understand life's circumstances. He takes you on a journey of how faith and a sense of meaning and purpose can help you move forward. I am truly excited that he has now put in writing his wisdom that helped so many people fact their lives with added strength.

Thank you very much, Chuck, Leo and Cheryl! Thanks for sharing your feelings, thoughts, and expectations for this book. You have all been an inspiration to me, and I have enjoyed sharing with you and benefiting from our experiences in the mental health field and in helping others in any way we could.

Dr. Marvin Johnson

Introduction

Throughout my life I have written numerous articles and given many presentations, but this is the first time I've collected my thoughts into a book. Since I've reached the age of 85, it will probably be my first and last! This book offers an overview, as much as possible, of what I have learned in my work, which has been dedicated to helping people solve life's problems and encouraging them to live life to its fullest. I have dealt with many issues during my 55 years of counseling individuals, families and groups, helping them solve mental health or relationship problems.

My education includes a Masters Degree in Social Work and a Doctorate in Psychology. This background has led me to work in different settings, all dealing with personal and family mental health problems. For 24 years I was a Division Chairman of the Social Work Department at Lutheran General Hospital, a major teaching Hospital in Park Ridge, Illinois. Following that I served as Program Coordinator for an in-patient psychiatric unit at Northwest Community Hospital in Arlington Heights, Illinois. After two years in that work I set up a private practice along with two other psychologists, where I worked fulltime for about twenty years. Then I retired, but was 'talked into' coming back part time for about another four years! Mine was a challenging career but also fulfilling, and I miss it a lot.

After retiring I became a volunteer for the Cancer Care Foundation, which provides free psychotherapy to Cancer patients and their families. This therapy could occur in the therapist's home, the patient's home, hospital or hospice. I felt I could be helpful to patients with terminal illness so also volunteered for a hospice called Journey Care. I see some of their hospice patients and also serve on their Ethics Committee.

This book will fall in the category of 'Self Help'. We know that no book can be of total help to its readers, therefore my goal has been to present some broad ideas and look at some specific problem areas, all of which I have dealt with in my career. Having worked with thousands of individuals, couples and groups to help identify and deal with their problems in the best way they can, I know that not all problems can be solved through psychotherapy, but many can be understood, clarified and improved, making life more fulfilling.

Some persons feel much better during and after counseling, some a little better, and some not much better. Successful 'self help' is determined by the person's understanding and interest in working on issues. Sadly, some have lost hope and may have little or no will to work on bettering their lives. Those who try hard can usually improve their lives or their situations and feel better and more fulfilled.

The chapters in the book cover problem areas that I have dealt with during my career. Depression and marital problems are the issues I have encountered most frequently, and those chapters are the longest. I am aware that entire books have been written about the problem areas I cover, and that my thoughts and actions will be less expansive. This book is primarily about my personal impressions, techniques, observations and psychotherapy techniques. I am not including any research or writings of others and have not utilized any Internet information. What readers will find is a bit of what I have learned, and some of my own ways of responding and attempting to help. What I offer is meant to be practical and realistic, not conjecture or philosophy, in the hope that the problem areas discussed will bring some help to individuals or couples who are struggling.

Another, and perhaps most important reason that I have put these thoughts together, is my desire to leave a legacy to my family. My family includes a beautiful wife, two wonderful daughters, four special stepchildren, their six caring spouses, and seven precious step-grandchildren. They all are included in my immediate family.

I also would like to leave a written legacy to extended family, friends and anyone who reads this book. I may or may not know you, but, if this book helps you in any way, it is my legacy to you also.

Often a legacy is thought of as practical things, like an inheritance of money or items of special value or emotional importance being passed on. The legacy I offer is meant to give ideas, and maybe help toward having a fulfilling and happy life by dealing with problems more quickly and openly. Ultimately, I encourage readers to work on the following: love God, love yourself, love others, give and help others, always try, never give up hope, have short and long-term goals, face your problems (real or emotional), try to make things better, find a purpose for living, share with others, do the best you can and accept what you cannot do. Make a difference while you enjoy the journey.

Finally, may my thoughts and experiences provide hope to persons who are struggling with difficult problems of a long duration, including some from childhood. Please remember that if an individual tries there is hope; at a minimum hope for improvement. I am not saying all mental health problems can be cured, but major issues, especially those with a genetic base, can be improved, and the person affected can deal with them in a more effective way.

Writing this book has been a challenge and a desire stemming back many years. Sitting down and doing it has been a kind of emotional release for me, as I have made a major effort to remember the facts and feelings of my career. It has brought back many memories, most fulfilling and satisfying but some sad as well. Looking back at my career I am not going to say to myself "Job well done," but am going to say, "I tried and did my best."

◊

1
Dealing with Mental Health Issues

As stated in the Introduction, I have spent my 55 years as a clinical psychotherapist trying to be of help to individuals, families and groups struggling with mental health issues. My graduate degrees, but even more so the thousands of patients I have talked to, have taught me a lot. I want to begin this book by expressing some general guidelines to help deal with those issues. Later chapters will be more specific with regard to problems and dealing with different areas of mental health.

I feel there are several activity guidelines that help a person cope with a mental illness; an adjustment disorder to a life event, social issue like marital or family problems, or any other kind of problem we find difficult to understand or resolve. Obviously therapy or medication may be required, but I will describe some other steps that can be taken for possible improvement. One thing that always helps is to identify the problem and clarify who has the problem. Often persons coming in for initial visits can't clarify why they feel as they do and what might be causing that feeling. They might complain because their spouse seems angry a lot but don't realize it is their own bad behavior that leads to the spouse's anger. Identifying the problem can be difficult and takes a lot of self-exploration and thought with minimum projection towards others.

It can help to try to share and discuss the problem or problems with trusted friends or family. Doing this is not intended for "therapy" but to get a better perspective on things and maybe some advice, direction, or understanding from others. Family and friends, who have had some of the same issues can also be helpful. Find and read appropriate self-help books or books that focus on your problem area. Books cannot totally personalize your specific concerns, as many problems have multiple dimensions, but they may give you new emotional areas to explore or things to try.

What is important is to try to take action. I have seen many patients who want to 'do something' to help solve their problems, and taking action can be helpful for them. It may not totally solve the problem, but it may help. One thing I have suggested for someone struggling with choices or who feels overwhelmed is to write out, on separate pieces of paper, possible options or things that could be attempted. Put them all into a box, attempt to turn off your thoughts about the dilemma if you can, and the next day open the box and take a 'fresh look' at your options. It can be surprising what you can accomplish if you give your problem a day off!

Spiritual resources, if desired and available, can be helpful. Saying a prayer quietly or out loud or turning in a prayer request at your house of worship helps give some peace of mind to a troubled person. It helps to feel the Higher Power is aware of your need and will do something to help. Reading spiritual books or journaling about your feelings can often give a bit more motivation and insight, which can be very helpful.

Meditation can be helpful as it can slow down your thought process and help you to relax. Quiet, thinking, deep breathing, guided imagery all distract you from the worrisome, stressful or depressive feelings you are having. You may need to take meditation training to use it most effectively. Many places offer that, often at low cost. There are also CDs available that help develop guided imagery skill.

Exercise and vigorous working out can help, especially with feelings of anger or stress. The inner tensions can be redirected to a treadmill, weights or even a boxing bag if available. These can turn your inner feelings, especially anger or stress, into aggressive exercise. It can help lessen the feelings and help you redirect your energy into a positive action.

Cognitive thinking can be an important area to consider. Most mental health issues are because of feelings we have about our life's situation. Social and marital problems are also greatly impacted by how we feel about things and the person involved. Insight may help to change feelings, but checking whether our feelings match the facts and reality of a situation can do even more. We can feel depressed, and anxious, partly because we misunderstand the reality of the situation. A more honest view of why we feel as we do helps change the feeling. We may feel a friend dislikes us but a factual and accurate view of the truth may be that your perception was incorrect. The new and correct facts help the feelings of dislike to go away or at least ease.

Life is full of changes we experience as good, bad or uncertain. Some change is wanted, others a surprise, some not wanted. But, in any case, change is a challenge and often difficult. Many writers, including Shakespeare, talk about stages of life. However it is defined, each stage is an adjustment often involving loss, new experiences, and change of many kinds. Part of dealing with life is to anticipate change as much as possible and to see it as an opportunity, not a loss. Some stages, such as growing older and retiring, require the most adjustment. I have seen hundreds of older people who have said, in various ways, "The Golden Years are not very golden for me!"

Why do some have more trouble with life's changes than others? Part of that answer is to look at that old question of "What shapes our lives? Is it heredity or environment?" The answer is that both are issues, but numerous recent researchers have emphasized that genetics may play a stronger role than we thought in the past, for an illness including mental health problems. If our view of the world is clouded by depression, anxiety, paranoid thinking or other issues, we will have problems coping with life's stages. If our current family life has lots of anger, neglect, violence, then of course that also impacts our ability to adjust to change.

It is also true that our personalities stay fairly consistent throughout all stages of our life. If we are self-assured at age 40, know how to deal with issues, seize opportunities, face life with hope, we will probably face older age with fewer problems.

On the other hand, if life has been a constant struggle, full of disappointment and failure, lots of losses, we will probably find the same challenges when we reach age 80 and beyond.

Everyone in life will face problems, some small and some big. Our goal is to focus on problem solving, not denying problems or blaming others. Psychotherapy does not totally change people or magically eliminate problems. Its goal is to provide understanding of problems and develop inner strength to help find the best ways to deal with issues, to reduce the pain or help persons learn to adjust and cope. We all need to feel understood and develop hope and a positive attitude about tomorrow and the future.

2
Depression

Depression is probably the most common among the mental health issues that I have dealt with in my career. It is very upsetting, as it can greatly affect qualify of life and emotional status in general. There are many types and levels of depression. The most serious one is Major Clinical Depression but there are also lower levels that can create problems. Situational Depression is related to a depressive situation in life – maybe the loss of a parent or other loss or sad or painful event in life. Normally Situational Depression lessens with time but often never goes away entirely.

One of the most challenging to deal with is a high level of Bi-Polar Illness. That is when a person suffers significant depression but often quite quickly switches to manic feelings with no depression. One of the problems with bi-polar is that often patients do not like the medication for it, as the meds take away the extreme highs. Often patients like the highs and the manic behavior that goes with it and don't like the mid-level of emotion that medication provides. I have heard bi-polar patients complain that their medication "takes away their personality."

So what do you do about depression? First, the problems need to be evaluated. Do you have mild, moderate or severe major depression, or situational depression? Is there an obvious reason for it? Do I have significant mood swings? Are there times when I am not depressed at all? Answers to those questions help clarify the plan of action.

Modern mental health specialists feel genetics are frequently a contributing factor, especially to Major Depression and Bi-Polar. In those cases, psychotherapy can help but medication will probably also be needed. Many therapists, including myself, try to utilize two aspects of therapy. The past is studied to see if there are past issues, events, or problems that affect current feelings and behavior. If so, those are processed to help the patient better understand what happened, see their role (if any) in those events, and to learn to deal with them in a better way.

An unusual but interesting example was a couple I was seeing and one of the issues was a historical event that affected the husband. We discussed it, and I made a comment about its possible connection to a current problem they were having. He pondered it for about a second, jumped up and said, "That's it, that's why I have this problem." His wife was surprised and said, "I only thought something like that happened in movies!"

The second task, after a review of past issues, is the cognitive therapy approach. This is to help the patient think about things in a different way. Our thoughts, and our interpretation of life, affect our feelings. If a person "feels" everyone looks down on him and thinks he is unworthy, then he is going to feel badly. But if he realizes his interpretations of life and persons are often not correct or exaggerated, and that actually many people like him, his feelings may change and he will feel better. I have pointed out to hundreds of people, "Feelings aren't necessarily Facts."

Not all depressed people confuse fact and feeling. Clinical depression can persist even though people are coping fairly well and managing the depression to attain some measure of adjustment. But most depressed persons do have a negative view of the world, like viewing life through grey-colored glasses. The cognitive approach can help with those distortions. Defining the problem correctly and looking at it in a problem-solving way are both vital, but so is helping the patient to be able to share their feelings, look at the problem with honesty, and develop energy and strength to deal better with the problem. The patient needs to trust the therapist and feel that he/she understands, cares and can help resolve problems. Insight and inner strength help in facing and reducing the power of the problem. Often the first time a patient has ever shared the deepest feelings or darkest past is in a therapy session, where they feel safe, understood and not judged.

The sad thing about a clinical (partially genetic) depression is that psychotherapy, insight, understanding and cognitive thinking can help to lessen the power, but the depression never goes totally away unless medication is also provided. Both are required for best results. Early in my training, I remember a psychiatrist stressing over and over that one of the major benefits for a patient is the "relationship." I agree it is very helpful for a person receiving therapy to feel understood and that the therapist cares no matter how bad, confused, scared or mixed-up the patient may be.

I feel that it helps if patients "DO" something in addition to talking and thinking. I will frequently assign homework and, for depression, the assignment is often to make a list of things about which they are depressed or list how depression is making their lives difficult. Part two of that homework is to list positives in their lives, things that make them happy and what they enjoy. Each item is reviewed to find ways of possibly improving on the depression list and ways to enjoy and react even more to the positive list. I feel hope and goals for the future are essential elements of a fulfilled life.

As mentioned, some persons with bi-polar do not like the medication, as they feel it makes them too "flat." They don't like the depression but can enjoy the manic phase even though they often do things to excess, which they later regret. Articles and books have been written that suggest some powerful people have benefited from being bi-polar. Churchill, Franklin Roosevelt and Lincoln are often used as examples, although there may not be "proof" of their diagnoses. The theory is that during depression the leaders felt the pain of their situation and the pain of the people they were responsible for helping. The manic phase gave them the motivation to come up with ideas to help and energy to implement positive change.

Depressed persons especially need a few basic things including hope and goals for the future. They need people they trust, with whom they can share; a challenging and fulfilling life with purpose and direction and some sense of accomplishment. It is also important to acknowledge and accept the limitations of depression but not let depression define who you are. Be the best that you can. There are times when depression seems to be triggered or enhanced by life events. The events may create different reactions but the most common ones are post-traumatic stress disorder, often found in war veterans; post-partum depression; and child abuse, including sexual abuse by a parent or a previously trusted adult. Some of these persons could be the clergyman, teacher, coach, neighbor, friend or family member.

Post-Traumatic Stress Disorder (PTSD) is a major problem for veterans, and news reports indicate that over twenty veterans a day commit suicide, most suffering from this diagnosis. In PTSD a person goes through a major crisis event or events that affect him/her deeply. The events are often life threatening, filled with fear and often beyond the person's control. After the event, often months after the event, emotions flood the person's mind such as fear, painful thoughts, memories, loss, even the feeling that life has no meaning and so on. It can occur especially if the person is going through difficult times at home, at work, or in their lives. Many of those with PTSD have a background of stress and problems in their lives while growing up. If those have not been understood and resolved, the PTSD may be more prominent.

Post-partum situations are complicated and difficult to predict and sometimes to understand. We all hope an exciting event like a new child will be welcomed with much positive anticipation and joy. Just the reverse can happen and can be very disruptive to a family. Some of the contributing factors could be a genetic predisposition to depression, which is triggered by the new birth. That predisposition can also be triggered by other major events or changes such as divorce, major loss, catastrophic illness and others. There are also hormonal changes that occur in the body after the birth that may be an issue as well. From the nine months of being careful, eating properly, taking care of herself to suddenly going through the rigors of childbirth can present difficult moments for any mother. Another issue is the major "life change" that occurs after a birth. There is a new child to care for, who cries and needs attention, possible breast-feeding challenges and lack of sleep, and huge new responsibilities.

Part of the dilemma of post-partum is that, in many cases, it is totally unexpected and therefore the mother is confused and puzzled. Also others expect the new mother to be happy, pleased, and excited about the new addition and may not understand or be sympathetic to a post-partum depression. It is especially difficult if the new child's father is not understanding of the mother's feeling and is not supportive of her struggles. Family understanding and support is very important for the mother with this affliction. The depression can be severe and, in our practice, there was a major awareness of the risk of suicide for the patients.

I remember one case where a patient suffering from post-partum depression phoned her therapist in our office and said, "Thank you for trying to help me." She did not elaborate on that statement as she was driving, and shortly thereafter purposely drove into a lake with her newborn and both died. The therapist was extremely upset, but the patient had not mentioned her intentions in any way in her therapy or in the phone call. Most of our post-partum patients preferred a female therapist, which we would provide at their request.

Child abuse and especially sexual abuse can also trigger depression and related problems in adulthood. There are times when those memories only surface to the patient's mind in therapy. In exploring the reasons for depression, such as low self-esteem, mistrust, and self-blame, the patient often "remembers" the abuses and then attempts to deal with them. Those who remember the abuse often were not able to deal with it as a child. Possibly their parents did not believe what they said or the adult denied it. Sometimes the adult was a prominent person, possibly in the eyes of the community, and they were afraid to say anything as they felt no one would believe and they would be criticized. Some were young enough that they didn't exactly understand what was going on, liked the attention of the adult, and only when they grew older did they really understand what had happened.

Sometimes the adult would say "nice" things and convince the child they had a "special secret" that should not be shared. Self-blame comes in if the child/adolescent feels that they did not protest or protest enough and are partially at fault. It is especially devastating if the child tries to tell a parent and is not believed, or worse, even criticized for saying what was said. Trust in adults is compromised and self-esteem suffers.

PTSD and post-partum often, not always, occurs in persons who have had incidents or issues in their past that are unresolved. Those issues may appear unrelated but actually are important, as they help shape how the person sees and faces life, adversity and change. It is obvious in child abuse that those events can seriously affect them in facing life and dealing with life's challenges as an adult.

In all cases there are some similar things that can be tried that may help. Of course therapy and medication should be considered when necessary. Sharing facts and feelings with trusted friends can be very helpful. Help your friends to realize that you may need to talk about your situation, especially your feelings, more than once. Some friends might get impatient if they hear things two or three times but let them know that it is important for you to share frequently. If there is someone who has abused or hurt you in some way try to talk to that person and share your anger, frustration, mistrust, if at all possible. If that is not possible, then write him/her a letter fully expressing how you feel and how their behavior hurt you. There is no requirement to mail the letter, even if you know the address. The important part is to write it down, and to express and clarify your feelings. If you are able, forgive them for what they did or didn't do.

It is also important to remember feelings do not always represent facts. Also remember who really has the problem in this situation. If you were abused, the abuser has the problem. You are the victim with feelings about their behavior. It is okay to be angry with them but not okay to blame yourself or feel guilty about the experiences. If you view the actual facts of some of your past problems, your feelings about them may change or mellow. Also "do something" if you are not able or cannot confront the people in your past that have caused problems. Take action of some other kind that expresses your feeling such as working-out aggressively. Tell them how you feel by yelling out loud, in a place that is comfortable for you, telling them how you feel. Writing their names on a paper and ripping it up with resoluteness can also assist you in facing your anger. These may sound silly, but any action that helps us express our inner hurt or angry feelings can be helpful.

Guided imagery can also help. There are CD's that can guide you in this, but you can do it yourself. In a quiet spot, relax and picture yourself in a place of love, peace and calmness. Don't do anything; just be there and turn off your real world briefly. Enjoy that escape place in your mind. You can go there often. Biofeedback is often used in somewhat the same way in some therapy sessions, but a machine is necessary to accomplish this. I have occasionally told patients to check the "off" switch as they begin their guided imagery.

Do whatever you can to let your feelings out in a way that they will be heard and accepted. Pray if that helps, join a sharing or therapy group, read a self-help book or two, and, if you can, keep busy. Take whatever action you can to fight the impulse to let depression control or influence your life and your behavior. Things are not solved or improved by sitting at home feeling bad and crying. Always try to find hope and things to live for, even if they are small. Then give yourself credit for "doing something." Goals and hope for the future are important and needed by all well functioning people.

3
Anxiety and Stress

There was a lot of stress and anxiety within the family in which I grew up. Our home was on a small farm in South Dakota, and during my childhood the country was experiencing the Great Depression. At home, our crops were often ruined by dust storms, drought or swarms of grasshoppers. I remember seeing my Dad with several other farmers shoveling dirt to improve a dirt road and being "paid" by the W.P.A. (the Government's Works Progress Administration which helped the poor.) My five siblings and I didn't realize until much later the amount of stress my parents had at that time. Our food was what we grew or raised on the farm. Leftovers, if any, were always eaten at the next meal, often in soup. We ate everything on the table, even if it wasn't our "favorite".

As a young adult, I began to realize the amount of stress they had gone through and also how they endured it. The community of farmers helped one another! We shared corn, chickens, and potatoes with neighbors, as they did with us. Everyone attended church, which became a hope for the future and an emotional support system. No one complained, everyone gave to others; we had faith and hope and love, and in time, things improved on all of the farms. I remember as an adult my brother once saying, "We were poor but we didn't know it, so it didn't matter!" Stress was not talked about or struggled with; life was accepted and endured.

Anxiety and Stress, to a degree, are part of all of our lives. It is "how much" of each that can present a problem. Anxiety and stress are usually found together. There is one diagnostic category called "Free Floating Anxiety" in which a person is anxious about most everything in their life. That is very common. If you are stressed about your work or parenting, you are no doubt also anxious about them. Some people feel stress is a more focused feeling – you are stressed about a specific area – while anxiety can be more general.

This chapter will mirror that concept. Stress will be presented as more focused and specific and anxiety more pervasive and general. Both are feelings, not necessarily "facts." One of the first things to do is to identify and acknowledge the feelings, and then do a reality test to see if your feelings are appropriate for the situation, or if they are overblown. Every personality is different. We all handle anxiety and stress in different ways and react to different degrees, with some persons being "worriers" and others being "nothing bothers me" types.

There is no precise standard for anxiety and stress. Anxiety about losing a job is not always rated a "10." The level of reaction depends upon the personality/nature of the person and the perceived change of life and finances if a job is lost. Stress, like depression, can be situational or more focused and therefore may be helped or diminished if the "situation" can be resolved or corrected. A parent has a terminal illness and is in Hospice, so anxiety about it would be realistic. A parent developing a cold usually would not warrant an anxiety attack or sleepless night. Freud has written that personality is consistent, meaning that if you have too much anxiety in one area of your life, you are likely to be anxious in many areas.

The most problematic part of dealing with these feelings is when your reactions are excessive, based upon what you are upset about. People with insecurities or those who have had traumatic things happen are more likely not to handle these feelings well. An extreme example would be the veterans returning, who have seen conflict, danger, maybe death. They may develop Post

Traumatic Stress Disorder (PTSD), and become overly anxious about most everything in their life.

Stress and anxiety can affect our life and emotions in many ways. Some of the more common problem areas are persistent worry, lack of sleep, and an impact on physical health. It can permeate or control your thoughts, may affect your judgment and decision-making, cause you to be unable to relax, cause fear of the future, or make you feel that life has lost its meaning. Having the above feelings, or some of them, means action must be taken to reduce or control the stress.

Volumes have been written about stress and a quick look on the Internet would probably give you dozens of "tips" to avoid or deal with those emotions. The following is an outline of stress management that I used for a series of lectures on stress. I think it is fairly self-explanatory and of course in the lectures, I expanded on each point, which I will also do, to some degree, in this chapter.

I. DEFINITION OF STRESS
    A. Chronic, life-style stress
    B. Event related stress
    C. Stress may trigger other emotions

II. REACTIONS TO STRESS
   A. Physical
   B. Emotional
   C. Both

III. WHAT IS MY STRESS AND AM I "OVERREACTING?" IF SO, WHY?
   A. Previous bad experience
   B. Perceptions of stress (perceptions may not be reality)
   C. Cognitive evaluation of stressors – realistic assessment
   D. Vulnerable point in life

IV. TAKING ADVANTAGE OF STRESS
   A. Use as motivator to take action
   B. Use to make positive changes in your life or in your life's circumstances

V. BAD WAYS TO COPE WITH STRESS
   A. Alcohol
   B. Food, especially "comfort" food
   C. Spending
   D. Over medicating
   E. Avoiding, denying, escaping, blaming

VI. GOOD WAYS TO DEAL WITH STRESS
   A. Know your limits: realistic expectation and positive attitude.

B. Focus on what you can control or change, not what you cannot.

C. Utilize your life experiences, i.e. how you have handled previous stress.

D. Take care of yourself: eat well, sleep soundly, take time to relax, exercise, and take walks.

The definition of stress is not as important as learning how to deal with it, but we do need to understand, at least a little, the problem we are attempting to control. Some research has shown that our ability to deal with stress is partly controlled by our genetic make-up and our developed personality. Some persons are more prone to be "stressed out," and it takes little stress for them to feel overwhelmed. Therefore stress cannot be defined by a single stressful event as people react differently to the same event.

Most stress is caused or worsened by a situation in a person's life. It could be practical, like money problems or emotional like marital problems or fear of divorce. In a general sense, stress is often increased or activated by change or loss. The change or loss may be an actual change of some kind – either positive or problematic – or an anticipated loss. Often the stress begins when the person anticipates the events and is stressed out long before anything actually happens. As mentioned, often positive and anticipated good changes can activate stress, as it makes our future a little uncertain and becomes stressful. Anticipating stress would be something like overly worried about retirement (20 years away) or getting married and worrying if the marriage will work.

Reactions to stress are obviously impacted by the intensity and duration of the stressful feelings. Extreme stress, even short term, can cause many physical and emotional reactions. Chronic unresolved stress can "grind" away at a person's feelings and cause numerous problems. Common feelings can be fear, insecurity, sadness, anxiety, withdrawal and reduced meaning and purpose in one's life.

Defining your stress can be challenging and difficult. We often judge things based on our view of life, and if we have had a number of unresolved stresses in the past, we probably will become stressed more easily than we would like. Our definitions of stress are guided by our perceptions and interpretations of the issues facing us. We need to be sure we understand and perceive correctly the issue of change worrying us, so our stress is appropriate for the event. We also need to keep in mind that our stage of life can be an issue and levels of vulnerability may also impact reactions to stress. As we age, we may be less resilient, and if we have other issues such as medical problems, relationship issues, parental concerns and so on, our resistance can be lowered and ability to cope lessened.

There may be times when we can use our feelings of stress as motivators to take action. Redirecting our feelings, including angry and stressful ones, can push us into action to "do" something and not just suffer in silence. Maybe we can change the situation or change our attitudes about it. Maybe there are positives we failed to see because our thoughts were clouded by stress. Let the intensity of the stress help you pull out coping resources and remind yourself that you have conquered problems and problem feelings in the past and can do it again.

There are several "bad" ways to deal with stress, and several are mentioned in the outline. Those are accurate and are especially bad if stress triggers them to excess, therefore creating additional problems. Of that group probably alcohol and drugs are the most used and the ones that can lead to numerous physical and emotional problems. Another common one in the listed group is denying or belittling your feelings. Internalizing those feelings allows them to "fester" and grow and eventually another small stressful event will cause an explosion of feelings, as they have been stored up for days or even months. Be honest, don't deny, don't postpone, talk to others, "do something," become a survivor. The previous outline listed ways to cope and several additional ones are added below. The major focus of this chapter is to identify and understand your stress and find positive things to diminish or control it.

Additional ways to deal with stress are:

1) Look at the facts of the situation and see if your feelings match those facts. Perceptions create feeling. If your view of the situation changes, your feelings about it will probably also change.

2) Check out your feelings with trusted friends or your spouse. Get their honest opinion about how you feel. If they agree and understand, accept their help and support and use that to help you cope. If they see the situation from a different perspective, consider their point of view.

3) We all learn from our past. If you have coped with stress previously, review what you did to

help manage the feelings. Be a survivor, don't be a victim.

4) Feel free to discuss your problem and feelings with a therapist if you feel the problem is getting too difficult to handle or even if you need assistance in using the other ways to deal with it.

5) Refocus your thoughts. One way to do that is to write out possible solutions or things to do about your situation, maybe a direction to go or some possible plans. Put the list in a box and do not think about it for a day. Often a visit to the list a day later will help your focus on what to do or which direction to move. Let your mind have a day off!

6) If possible, take a break and do something actively physical or energetic. Focus on your exercise, push yourself, and attempt to divert your thoughts.

7) Do something symbolic: It may seem strange but sometimes helps. One would be to write down your stress and anxiety on a sheet of paper, put the sheet in a paper bag and aggressively tromp on it, tear it up and put it in the garbage. Let the feelings go!

8) Focus on areas of your life that are okay, things you love, what you have accomplished, people who care, and things that are going well. Try to find humor in something; laugh if you can.

9) If you are spiritual, pray to God for help. Trust you are heard and that God loves you and is on your side and will give you strength or direction.

10) Divert your attention, attend a movie or a concert, read a book, visit with friends, take up a hobby or take a class on something you enjoy.

11) Look at your life in a total perspective. How important is this feeling of stress? Life is a journey; it will end down the road. Make the most of all the good stuff and try to put up with and cope with the troublesome things.

12) Try to find goals to work toward to help with the stress. List them and try to do them as soon as your can and when you have done one, give yourself a "pat on the back" and feel good. Some goals may take a longer time but when done, rejoice. Redirect your energy.

13) Keep a journal and write your feelings daily. By the same token, share your ongoing feelings with people who care and love you.

14) Get enough sleep, eat well, don't try to compensate by over-drinking alcohol to dull the feelings, as that usually only makes it worse.

15) Do what you can and try to accept what the result may be. Don't just "sit in a corner and cry." Be creative, thoughtful, imaginative, and persistent. Take action and always remember that in a stressful situation, while you may or may not be able to change the situation, you can change yourself and your feelings about it.

16) Try not to fall into the "why me?" trap. A cancer patient, a young lady with two children, came in, with her husband, for help in dealing with her terminal illness. Early in our work I asked her if she had any angry or "why me" thoughts. She pondered briefly and said, "No... my feeling is 'Why not me?' I'm no better than anyone else, and we must all deal with life as it is." She maintained that perspective until her death.

17) Stress is an emotion. Try to direct your feelings to other areas or activities such as a church or community group, a self-help or growth organization, or anything positive that you like and can direct feelings to and get good feedback. Local libraries or senior centers often have interesting groups for the public to attend.

18) Learn to relax, take yoga, go to a meditation group, go to a prayer group, sit in silence and focus on peace and quiet, get a massage, listen to soft relaxing music, take a nap or a walk in the park, play with your pet. Determine what your reality is in a stressful situation and learn to cope and make the most of what you have. Don't grieve for what you may not have. Try to turn the stress switch off and relaxation on.

19) To sum it up... life is short! Don't sweat the small stuff; play the cards you have been dealt; don't grieve the past or fear the future – live for today and make the most of each day.

A technique I used a lot in therapy sessions related to stress and anxiety is biofeedback with guided imagery. Biofeedback utilizes a machine that connects to the patient's finger and records pulse rate. I would connect the patient to the machine, have them relax on the sofa, eyes closed, head tilted back. I would then describe for them a beautiful summer day in a field by a quiet stream, green trees around, birds chirping, lying on a blanket, no cars, planes, trains, only peace and quiet out in the country. Almost all the time the patient's pulse rate slowed and they were able to temporarily turn off the "real" world for a brief visit to a place of peace and quiet. I have had several patients who became so relaxed they fell asleep and many who didn't want the guided imagery to end. The guided imagery technique works just as well without the Biofeedback machine, and, in most of my sessions I did not use the machine.

Stress is common to all ages, but I have probably seen it most pronounced in the Senior Citizen stage of life. Often persons who have had emotionally satisfying careers find retirement more difficult. Trying to replicate your career by selective volunteering can help, but the adjustment is often difficult. There are many things that are either over or have changed. Physical health may be a worry, financial concerns an issue, children are grown up and don't need you as they did, activities that were fun can't be done. For many the focus is on what the wonderful and fulfilling past was rather than enjoying the current retirement stage.

The concerns are usually health and illness and fear of being alone and lonely. Many older persons have said their biggest stressor is fear of becoming dependent, either on children or needing to be cared for in a nursing home or similar. I remember one elderly woman who was very depressed about her situation saying, "I'd like to commit suicide, but I'm afraid I might not do it successfully and would then be in even worse shape than now." Aging can be complicated by physical health and memory issues as well, which cause stress for the person and often stress for their children.

Focus on life and your journey in its totality. Stress is often a part, but so can love, joy, hope, goals, achievements be a part of it. Focus on those positive aspects. Put stress in the back room of your mind and lock the door! Look at the facts of the situation and see if your feelings match those facts. Perceptions create feeling. If your view of the situation changes, your feelings about it will probably change as well.

4
Suicide and Suicidal Thoughts

Many seriously depressed people think about
suicide when they are under stress and times are
especially difficult, but there are many other
problem times that thoughts of suicide may occur.
Anger is often as issue, as are mental health
problems such as paranoid ideation, feelings of
being lonely, unloved and disliked, and feelings of
being rejected. Loss of hope, seeing no future or
even guilt about the past can contribute.
Sometimes suicide can be triggered by major
traumatic situations in life. Death of a significant
person such as a spouse or child, loss of job,
development of a major illness, excessive pain,
chronic illness and dependency can all be triggers.
If suicidal thoughts have been present before,
sometimes these problems can exacerbate serious
suicidal planning or action.

Most therapists, including myself, feel partially to
blame if a patient attempts or completes a suicidal
act. Some patients I have seen have a history of
suicidal thinking, so, of course, you are more
aware and cautious. Our psychological practice
had forms for "possibly" suicidal patients to
complete. They agree to not act on the feelings but

either call the therapist, 911, an immediate family member, or go to an Emergency Room. Verbally I have told patients thinking of suicide "Do not do it! Promise me you will take one or more of the steps outlined on the form that you signed."

Three suicides are still in my mind, even though their events were several years ago. A school teacher came in suffering from depression and feelings of failure. The feelings were described as moderately severe and suicide was never mentioned. He came in for two sessions and did not show up for his third. I called, as I always did, to find out what happened and to probably reschedule. A relative answered the phone and said he had committed suicide that morning. I was extremely shocked and began much soul searching. For whatever reason, he had not shared the depth of his feeling or his suicidal thoughts. That reinforces the concept that it is important to tell someone you trust what the depth of your feelings are and to share that with a therapist if you are in therapy.

A man, mid-60's, was referred to me by his psychiatrist. He had developed advanced lung cancer and his physician had sent him to a psychiatrist for meds. He was an unskilled laborer who had struggled to earn a living, and his life had been unhappy. His first question to me was "What are you going to do to help me?" I discussed the therapy goals. We would try to help him cope, make the most of his life, and help him deal with his illness in the best way he can. He did not really seem to think that that would help and kept on the "What are you going to do" theme. I called his psychiatrist, as I felt he needed stronger meds, which she immediately prescribed. I saw him two more times and the theme continued to be how I was going to help him. He was continuing his chemo and radiation, which were also unpleasant. Sometime after the third session, he went to his apartment, knelt by his bed and shot himself. He had very little family, and they were not surprised by his behavior. Obviously, he was not tuned into his emotional feelings about his cancer but only on the disease itself. He also had no "hope" and the quality of life was not an issue for him... only the quantity.

The third patient was a complicated situation. The couple had come in for marital counseling, and we had maybe three or four sessions, when the counseling took a dramatic turn. The couple came in, and the husband said to me that his wife had some information to share. The smiling, but serious, lady said she was the mother of Jesus and was glad about it. I asked a few questions to make sure she was serious and then arranged admittance to an inpatient psychiatric ward. I worked with her and her psychiatrist, and she had about a two-week hospital stay. She was, of course, on medication and had seen the psychiatrist every day. We again continued the marital work after her discharge, and, at the second session she came in looking very bright and reasonable. She said she had never felt better; that she was looking forward to a better life and all was "great!" I was surprised but pleased and affirmed her on her progress. We scheduled a time for the next week, but a day or two after our session she went into her basement and took multiple bottles of pills, which caused her death.

I selected these three situations because they represent the variety of issues causing suicidal thoughts and planning. In the first, the gentleman did not share the depth of his feelings. It is very important to share those feelings with a trusted friend, a clergyman, or a therapist. Bearing that burden alone can be devastating.

In the second case, the patient was focused on his lung cancer, and the emotional coping piece was misunderstood and maybe not even wanted. He wanted his illness cured or at least modified, and that was all that was important. He was aware the cancer would probably lead to his death down the road, and that was his total focus. Coping with it was not his plan and suicide became the escape.

The third shows how mental illness can be a factor in suicide. The marital problems were not major and were also impacted by her mental health. Her post-hospital "recovery" is in the psychology books but was the first time I had seen it so clearly. Her feeling of happiness and excitement was because she had made the choice for suicide and that choice made her happy and peaceful. Her problems were over! All the marital discord was done. She had found a way out! Her psychiatrist and I discussed her choice after her death, and he agreed that her planned suicide had been the answer to all her problems and it made her happy. This case points out how mental health can affect our thoughts, behaviors, and the actions we take to resolve them.

Part of the job of a good therapist, or even a good friend, is to be able to look beyond what people say and, instead, search out who they really are and what they really feel. Creative listening is a skill we all need. People are not always how they look or what they initially say. I once had a nationally known comedian come in for therapy after a brief hospital stay. I commented about the differences between his career of making people laugh and bringing joy to their lives and his inner feelings of significant depression. He commented that many, if not most, of the comedians he knows suffer from some level of depression. The comedy part is a way of coping and covering up sadness and lack of joy in their own lives.

As therapists, we are aware that suicidal thoughts and, to a degree, feelings are not uncommon. The danger is when the patient has the feeling and is developing the "plan" of action. The "plan" piece is the trigger. I have asked many patients to promise to call me or take other positive action, if they are seriously thinking of implementing their plan. I have often been very direct and said, "Don't do it!" regarding suicide. That promise from them has at times been inconvenient for me, including a call while being in the audience of a Chicago Symphony performance. When called, the person informed me he had just had a fight with his wife and that she had left. He initially refused to tell me what he had done but finally admitted he had taken a bottle of aspirin and other medications. He would not call 911 and initially would not give me his address. I insisted and finally he did give it to me, and I called the Police. He was hospitalized and his life was saved. I missed out on the symphony but was affirmed of the need for patients to make "the promise" to call. I was pleased to know that it had kept him alive.

A current issue in suicide in recent years has been the issue of assisted suicide. Several states and foreign countries now allow this. States in the USA all require certain conditions such as residency, Doctor's reports, and the history of the problem. It is interesting that studies show many persons who are approved do not actually take action. For them, probably knowing they have a way out gives them strength to hold on a little longer and lets them know that they now have a choice. I believe assisted suicide should be available under certain conditions, such as uncontrolled pain, or terminal illness.

The concept of suicide is viewed very differently, depending upon your situation in life. Persons who are majorly depressed, paranoid, feeling lonely, believing that no one really cares, having no hope, no joy in life, believing they have no future; these persons may see suicide as a "way out"! They believe their problems will be done, there will be no more pain, they will be free... and their only worry is to make sure the suicide attempt is successful. They worry they may still be alive but disabled, brain damaged, in pain, and still there will be no relief. That is why many suicide attempts involve two methods such as pills and carbon monoxide. Men and women often choose different methods, women choosing pills, men often something more aggressive such as guns, positioning in front of a train or hanging. Some feel suicide is a sin and that they may not go to Heaven if successful. Others don't want to disappoint or hurt family or friends with their choice, which discourages their taking action.

There is no absolutely guaranteed way to make sure a friend, relative or patient does not commit suicide. Those who are spiritual and find strength in prayer and belief in God or a Higher Power can be helped by that resource. Sharing honest feelings with a trusted person, the Higher Power included, can be essential in gaining strength to cope with what seems to be the overwhelming difficulties of life.

Many people contemplating suicide feel there is no other choice for them. They may have tried various options but feel that none have really worked. The person planning a suicide needs hope, understanding, love, and some plans for the future. The cure for suicide is "Don't do it;" look for meaning and purpose so you can move toward a happier and more fulfilling life. Let the suicidal feelings be a trigger to begin that search.

5
Marriage Problems

Individuals or couples who come to therapy for marital help are very common, with almost half of all my patients presenting this issue. It is usually more helpful if both attend the sessions, but there are times when one (often the male) refuses to attend and doesn't want to talk to some stranger about his feelings or the situation.

Early in the therapy, I ask them to prepare their marital problem list. There are times when I will suggest, or they ask, for an individual session or two for each of them. These can help clarify hidden issues, such as an affair for either, or some other secret that somehow needs to be dealt with. In cases where there are threats or intimidations, a private session may free up the person to be more honest with me and hopefully later with the spouse. The rule is that the individual sessions are private and not shared by me to the other, but the individuals are free to tell each other as much, or as little, as they wish.

For those who come in together, I follow a usual protocol. We try to define the problems in the marriage, discuss who has the problem, clarify motivation to work on the problems and establish goals. Issues of how they feel toward each other, levels of trust or mistrust, anger or blame, suspicion or fear – all will be evaluated as we move into the problem list and efforts at problem solving. The problem lists do not usually identify if one or the other has the problem but more so that it exists with the marriage.

The following are several true examples of problem lists identified early in the therapy by several couples. Their names are obviously not identified and the problems mentioned are from my therapy notes. You will see some common areas such as conflict, but each couple has their own special list and special needs.

Couple #1:
Communication bad
Conflict/Anger management
Different personalities
Not sensitive to other's needs
Not able to work together
Trust missing
No priorities

Couple #2:
Conflict management
Communication

Overreact to things
Lack of forgiveness
Belittle each other/name calling
Parenting
Extended family
No team concept
Bring up past problems
Disagree on finances

Couple #3:
Communication
Separate paths
Different priorities
Lack of personal healthcare
Stress
Role issues
Alcohol abuse

Couple #4:
Not close, not bonded
Only roommates
Don't confront problems
Don't show love/feelings
Different values/goals
Distant emotionally/not feel loved

Couple #5:
Conflict issues
Not enough time together

Need to talk more
Finances
Anger management
Need forgiveness for past issues
No partnership
Defensive when discussing issues
No intimacy

Couple #6:
Communication/no time to talk
Not together much
Anger
Drinking
Feeling alone
Extended family issues
Forgiveness needed for past things
Fight/name call/scream
Conflict management
Parenting
Not open with each other
No intimacy/emotional/physical
No respect

Often the "problems" are not obvious and frequently not clarified or understood by the couple. For the couples that have difficulty identifying issues, differ on the issues or don't understand the emotional impact of issues, I developed a paper and pencil evaluation tool.

This evaluation was made by me, is not published or copyrighted, so it can be used by anyone. The goal is for the couple to complete it separately and then compare results when completed. They need to discuss the answers at a quiet time, when they are not rushed for time. Each question should be discussed at length if necessary and not argued over. The goal is to understand strengths, areas they agree, but more important to identify problem areas to be discussed at home or in therapy. The tests are often brought to a therapy session if there are significant differences or areas of misunderstanding.

MARITAL EVALUATION

Rank answers from 1-5, with 1 being NO to 5 being YES.

Communication:
Do we talk enough about smaller practical issues i.e. "What's for dinner?" or "What do we want to do this week?"
[NO] 1 2 3 4 5 [YES]
Do we talk about emotional feeling issues i.e. hopes, dreams, fears, joys?
[NO] 1 2 3 4 5 [YES]

Do we have private feelings that are hard for us to share?

[NO] 1 2 3 4 5 [YES]

Have we worked out our individual roles in the marriage?

[NO] 1 2 3 4 5 [YES]

Have we managed issues such as who is in control, decision-making?

[NO] 1 2 3 4 5 [YES]

Are we able to compromise when necessary?

[NO] 1 2 3 4 5 [YES]

Do we manage well the more significant practical issues of money management, home maintenance, household upkeep?

[NO] 1 2 3 4 5 [YES]

Are we able to discuss issues without the issue becoming a win/lose?

[NO] 1 2 3 4 5 [YES]

Can I be totally honest about my feeling when we have differences?

[NO] 1 2 3 4 5 [YES]

Conflict Resolution:

Are we able to discuss, understand and resolve our differences easily?

[NO] 1 2 3 4 5 [YES]

Can we manage and control our arguments?

[NO] 1 2 3 4 5 [YES]

Do we use our conflict in a constructive problem-solving way?
[NO] 1 2 3 4 5 [YES]
Are we able to not let conflicts end up in anger and arguing?
[NO] 1 2 3 4 5 [YES]
Are we able to avoid having conflict over insignificant issues?
[NO] 1 2 3 4 5 [YES]
Do we resolve our conflict/anger by the end of each day?
[NO] 1 2 3 4 5 [YES]

Social/Family:
Do we have enough couple friends?
[NO] 1 2 3 4 5 [YES]
Do we get along well with our extended family?
[NO] 1 2 3 4 5 [YES]
Do we spend enough time socializing with family or friends?
[NO] 1 2 3 4 5 [YES]
Are our individual interests or activities understood or accepted by the other?
[NO] 1 2 3 4 5 [YES]
Is trust an issue in our relationship?
[NO] 1 2 3 4 5 [YES]
Is anger an issue in our relationship?
[NO] 1 2 3 4 5 [YES]

Do we have enough fun, joy and enjoyment in our marriage?
[NO] 1 2 3 4 5 [YES]
Do we have compatible interests and activities?
[NO] 1 2 3 4 5 [YES]

Marital Growth:
As our marriage has developed, are we growing closer?
[NO] 1 2 3 4 5 [YES]
Are we as much in love as we were?
[NO] 1 2 3 4 5 [YES]
Do we show love to each other?
[NO] 1 2 3 4 5 [YES]
Do we show appreciation to each other?
[NO] 1 2 3 4 5 [YES]
Do we say "Thank you" enough?
[NO] 1 2 3 4 5 [YES]
Do we look forward to time alone together?
[NO] 1 2 3 4 5 [YES]
Have we developed common interests and activities?
[NO] 1 2 3 4 5 [YES]

Intimacy:
Is our sex life satisfactory?
[NO] 1 2 3 4 5 [YES]
Do we talk about our sexual needs and interests?
[NO] 1 2 3 4 5 [YES]

Do we have intimate, close, times without having to have sex?
[NO] 1 2 3 4 5 [YES]
Do we hug enough?
[NO] 1 2 3 4 5 [YES]
Do we lovingly touch enough?
[NO] 1 2 3 4 5 [YES]
Are we playful in a loving, sometimes sensual, way?
[NO] 1 2 3 4 5 [YES]
Do we say "I love you" often or enough?
[NO] 1 2 3 4 5 [YES]
Do I love my spouse as much as I feel I should?
[NO] 1 2 3 4 5 [YES]
Do I think my spouse loves me?
[NO] 1 2 3 4 5 [YES]
I will work hard to improve our marriage, if it is necessary.
[NO] 1 2 3 4 5 [YES]
Do I think my spouse would work hard to improve our marriage?
[NO] 1 2 3 4 5 [YES]

Priorities:
Do you feel you are the most important person in your spouse's life?
[NO] 1 2 3 4 5 [YES]
Do you and your spouse agree on marital priorities and goals?

[NO] 1 2 3 4 5 [YES]
Do you discuss and make plans for your long-term goals as a couple?
[NO] 1 2 3 4 5 [YES]
Do you feel appreciated and loved by your spouse?
[NO] 1 2 3 4 5 [YES]
Does your spouse take what you say or suggest seriously?
[NO] 1 2 3 4 5 [YES]
Do you work to find private times together despite your hectic lives?
[NO] 1 2 3 4 5 [YES]
Does your spouse understand your needs in the relationship and try to meet them?
[NO] 1 2 3 4 5 [YES]
Do you show appreciation for the things your spouse does to contribute to the marriage?
[NO] 1 2 3 4 5 [YES]
Does your spouse show appreciation for the things you contribute to the marriage?
[NO] 1 2 3 4 5 [YES]

Summary:
List 5 things you enjoy about your marriage.
1.
2.
3.
4.
5.

List 5 things you could work on to improve your marriage.

1.

2.

3.

4.

5.

List 5 things you would like your spouse to work on to improve your marriage.

1.

2.

3.

4.

5.

The problem a couple presents can be divided into two related but broad categories. The first is behavioral problems such as he/she drinks too much, yells a lot, won't help around the house, is tight with money, and other identifiable issues. The second is harder to define but in many ways more difficult. It has to do with emotions such as trust, anger, suspicion, fear, or not being able to share feelings. Problem solving must deal with both of these groups and success (or lack of) will also be guided by the individual and couple's goals and willingness for both to work on those goals. If love and caring has faded, if one (or both) want out of the relationship, if reasons for staying have to do with fear or insecurity, then the future is uncertain. Both must look at their own contributions and not just blame the other. Any of these complicate the problem, and that is why trying to clarify and establish common goals is important.

For those couples whose goals are to resolve issues and improve their relationship, there are several areas that commonly appear and often become the focus of problem solving. These issues often look at the emotional parts of the problem. For example, if a wife yells too much at her husband, the answer is not "stop yelling": It is why that behavior occurs and what can be done to find a better solution. Because problems may occur in the following areas, I have labeled them the Ten Commandments for a Fulfilling Marriage:

1. Conflict Management
2. Constructive Listening
3. Communication
4. Control
5. Compromise
6. Cuddle and Touch
7. Climate of Supportive Behavior
8. Common Goals
9. Creative Thinking
10. Care and Maintenance of Marriage

My thoughts about the "10 Commandments" are as follows:

1. Conflict Management:

Any and all marriages have differences of opinion and behavior expectations. The goal is not a 'perfect' relationship but a harmonious, loving and problem-solving situation. Conflict issues are very common in problem marriages, and I have seen hundreds of couples where conflict is a major issue. There are a few guidelines for lessening or eliminating conflicted situations.

Never draw absolute lines in the sand or give ultimatums.

The goal is to resolve the issue, not to win or lose.

Do not use judgmental words such as "You are wrong," "You are mean, stupid, selfish," "You never do anything right." Problems are not resolved when a "You should, you always, or you never!" is utilized. That is judgmental and usually provokes an angry response.

Instead use "I" statements with an emotion attached. "I felt hurt when you said I was stupid."

"I felt sad when you forgot to call me as promised." "I felt angry when you called me lazy." Always use "I" words, which don't imply judgment and then express your feelings on whatever the upsetting event was.

Deal with the conflict as soon as possible. Try not to discuss conflict issues when you are most upset. Wait until you 'cool down' and then, in a more relaxed setting, discuss the issue openly.

Remember, we all have a right to our feelings but not a right to force them upon others. Also how we convert our feelings into behavior may also be an issue needing resolution. Feeling hurt doesn't mean you have a right to hurt the other person or feeling angry doesn't need to be expressed by loud yelling, cursing, or blaming.

Focus on one issue at a time. Don't try to work out all areas of conflict at one time. If there are more than one, develop a priority so issues don't get mixed up or magnified.

Unresolved long-term conflict can be very destructive. Internalized issues build up and turn into deeper feelings of anger, no peace of mind, lack of sleep, or physical health reactions. Emotional withdrawal can happen, and resentments permeate your relationship. With unresolved feelings, it can often lead to an over-reaction to a small issue. Conflict can be about behavior or about emotional issues. In any case the emotional sharing, on both sides, helps lead to an understanding and hopefully a better relationship. The goal is not to change anyone's 'personality', as we are somewhat stuck with that, but to change problem behavior or attitudes.

Underlying conflict resolution should be an honest desire to resolve issues and to feel loved and cared for in the process. Remember, the goal is not to control someone else's behavior but to control your own and try to influence your partner to review behavior that is upsetting to you.

Conflict resolution discussions should lead to action and not words alone. If the sharing reveals that 'person A' is not handling his or her responsibilities around the home, and 'person A' agrees, then there should be an action plan with brief reviews every few days. Talk is cheap but action is productive! Changes are easier if you are in a loving relationship, feeling loved and loving your spouse and feeling that your efforts are being encouraged and supported.

2. Constructive Listening:

Many issues are magnified, and magnified issues often create conflict because they are misunderstood. Listening to a person's comments is not necessarily understanding them or perceiving their real meaning. If we instantly react to what we 'thought' we heard, it is often an overreaction or an inappropriate one. It is fine to ask for clarification of a statement or of a person relating an incident, i.e. "I'm not sure I know what you mean," "How did it make you feel," "Are you saying you think I did something wrong."

We also sometimes hear things based on previous communications where it the previous communication really isn't the issue. The goal of constructive listening is to be sure your response is appropriate for the issue. It is hard to resolve an issue or problem if it isn't being discussed with a clear understanding.

We also can get caught-up in false expectations. If we feel our spouse is too critical, then it is easy to 'hear' criticism even when it is not intended. We often hear what we expect to hear, not necessarily what is meant.

3. Communication:

Feelings need to be shared in conflict resolution but also need to be shared when conflict is not an issue. If someone says, "I had a bad day and am upset," the issue should not only be what happened but how upset is the person. Part of a good relationship is to be 'tuned in' to your own feelings and share, but also to be tuned in to your partner's feelings and ask what they are.

Couples should have times when feelings about each other and the marriage are purposely reviewed. Certainly not weekly or even monthly but for sure on an anniversary or when a major event occurs, such as serious illness of a family member, death of a parent, or any major event that impacts both. I also feel it is helpful for couples to have a date night, at lease two to three times a month. Part of the night could be a quiet dinner, where they can catch up with life and discuss or plan with privacy. This is especially true if there are children or a life-style that keeps both busy with other things.

Sharing feelings does not guarantee that your partner will have the same feelings about a situation. If feelings about something are different, be sure the issue of disagreement is clearly understood. Feelings are partially based upon our interpretation of the event or issue. Remember feelings are never wrong... they are yours and you have a right to them; but others persons may not see it the same way. Feelings are often changed when a person has a different view of the facts of a situation. Understand the issue or event more completely and your feelings may be changed. All feelings should be shared in a meaningful relationship, not just those necessary for problem resolution. "I love you" should be a feeling often expressed, so should "I missed you at work today," or "I am so glad you are my spouse." Positive feelings feel good, build a more solid loving relationship, and bring more joy and peace to a relationship.

4.   Control and Controlling Behavior:

The "I am right and you are wrong" game is easy to play as it gets us "off the hook" for a problem as well as notifying your spouse that he/she has done a bad thing and is at fault. It is easier to find fault/blame with others than to evaluate our own behavior regarding an issue. There are certainly times when a spouse does something wrong or misunderstands you and does something hurtful. If that happens, think about a couple of things before you blame. Did he/she do "it" on purpose, were they careless, were they mad at you? Was it a mistake or purposeful? Next, look at yourself. Did I do anything to complicate this situation? Maybe I wasn't clear about something, maybe I had a bad day and am oversensitive, maybe I misinterpreted the "blame" thing my spouse did. Sometimes we blame our spouse for things that are our own responsibility. I have heard many complaints such as "my spouse makes me feel insecure," or "it is my spouse's fault that I am overweight," or "my spouse makes me feel nervous in public." A patient once said in a session, "Just remember, if you hold out your arm and point a finder at someone, you have three fingers pointing back at you." If is easy to criticize, blame, find fault with others, but it is more important, and more difficult, to evaluate your own behavior and accept your share of the "blame" in a situation.

5. Compromise:

Anger is a normal healthy emotion, which if expressed or handled badly, can cause mental stress and problems. One of the most common misuses of anger I have seen is when persons have allowed anger to be stored up or unexpressed and then they overreact to a minor disagreement. Not every episode regarding anger should be worth having a major fight about. Not every issue couples have conflict about is life or death, or is earth-shaking. Problems and differences can range from 1 to 10 and not all conflict should fall into the 10 range. Learn to gauge reactions to the importance of the issue. Remember issues can build up if not resolved and a 1 issue can grow to a 6 if other issues are added to it and all are unresolved. Also consider the feelings of your partner. If in a conflict situation, they have a level of 9 in their feelings and you have a level of 1, this difference should be considered. Not that you should always 'give up', but intensity of feelings should be a part of the compromise or resolution.

As previously written, many marital anger situations involve issues ranked 1 to 3 but are built up because of other unresolved inner issues. One way to reduce unresolved inner issues is to discuss angry feelings at the time of the event or as soon as it is possible. Do not store it up! The sayings "Let not the Sun go down on your wrath" or "Never go to bed angry" are correct. Another thing couples should try to do is to turn anger into positive action! A simplistic example might be a wife who is angry because her husband doesn't help around the house or puts things off. If she expresses her anger in a positive way, the husband hopefully will not become defensive, will see and understand her point of view, and will improve.

The goal of anger should be to improve and change a problem situation... not to convince the spouse how bad they have been and how wrong they are. It is very bad to turn anger into negative behavior such as yelling, swearing, threatening, throwing things or walking out. All are negative behaviors and only make the situation worse. Who can yell the loudest is not an answer to an angry situation. Talking about anger as soon as it occurs is great but if your inner feelings are almost out of control, it may be better to hold off until you have 'cooled down' a bit. Then at a more quiet controlled time express your feelings in a problem-solving way. If the issue has aroused angry feelings, and when the issue has been resolved or at least clarified, then a 'kiss and make up' time is appropriate.

Anger does not mean hate or I don't love you. Don't let anger mean more than it should. Most of the time you can be angry about what your spouse says or does, or what they don't do or say, but that doesn't mean you don't like or love the person. You might not like a husband's choice of words or actions, which is his 'behavior' but may still love him as a person. Who is right and who is wrong or trying to win so you don't lose are not problem-solving attitudes. Also, no one is perfect and accepting the others as they are is also part of the solution.

Always remember not to deny or suppress anger but express it appropriately and in a manner that expresses your feelings in a problem identification and problem-solving way. The goals of anger should be problem identification, action and problem resolution. Willingness to utilize compromise, negotiation, and bargaining in a spirit of love and relationship is essential.

6. <u>Cuddle and Touch</u>:

When intimacy in a marriage is discussed, it is often related to sex. Sex is a reflection of a couple's level of intimacy and should be a significant part of a healthy relationship. The focus here is to agree sexual life is important, should be rewarding and fulfilling for both and should be discussed if all a problem. But it is also important to look at other additional types of intimacy needed for a fulfilling marriage. Touching, not necessarily sexual or seductive, can be a part of experiencing intimacy. Touching a cheek, a shoulder, a quick kiss for no reason, a spontaneous hug, holding hands often, especially if out in public, are all ways of feeling closeness. A nice back rub after a hard day or a soft shoulder massage can help a couple feel close. Verbal comments can also reflect intimacy. "Can I help you with that," "Are you feeling okay," "I love you," "You look beautiful/handsome" are all reflecting closeness and intimacy. Actions also can help, such as a small gift for no reason, special surprise for a birthday, volunteering to help your spouse with a special issue or problem, going out of your way to do things that help the other person feel your care, you love for them and a desire to make their life better.

7. Climate of Supportive Behavior:

To be emotionally or practically supportive you need to know your partner's wants and needs, and where support is especially important. You need to be aware of the areas you and your spouse are working on so you can assist verbally or be supportive in other ways. Being supportive does not mean that you support your spouse in every behavior but you do in the ones important to him or her. Neither should you expect your spouse to understand and support you in areas where they may have different feelings than you do. Your support, when there, will influence a positive outcome. Part of any relationship is to realize there may be differences and if possible those should be coordinated and worked out. But no relationship is perfect, and often one has to accept that their partner has different feelings and accept those differences. Obvious examples might be who to vote for, which church to attend, and which parenting methods to use.

Knowing the personality needs of your spouse also helps you to know areas where you should especially be supportive. If your spouse feels often insecure, doubts their abilities, holds back, you need to provide special support for achievements, and positive behaviors. If they are controlling and demanding, you would especially support when they listen and cooperate around issues and discuss their behavior with them in a problem-solving manner.

8. Common Goals:

Establishing goals in a marriage can be complicated as you have his goals, her goals and our goals. Children or extended family issues may complicate any of these. Individual goals do not need to be the same as your spouse's, but they should be complimentary to the relationship. Also individual goals may be delayed, or rotated, depending upon the situation. If both want to finish their college degrees at the same time, the money involved and timing may not make that realistic. Couples need a combination of short-term goals and long-term. Long-term goals are usually issues such as saving for retirement, investment issues, when we think we may retire, possibly health issues. Short-term include purchases of items, planning vacations, charitable contributions, remodeling parts of a home and related things that require joint decision making. An important issue is to try not to let individual goals dominate your marriage or your spouse's life. Goals, even individual, should be discussed and hopefully endorsed.

Goals may change depending upon circumstances and also stages of life. Goals at twenty-one are not going to be the same as goals at seventy-one. A problem often seen with goals is that one partner feels his/her personal goals are more important than their spouse. Remember, marriage is about compromise, not winning. Being selfish or demanding does not usually benefit a relationship.

Some goals regarding personality differences can also be difficult. She wishes to have a more active social life, more friends, more dinner parties, but he is socially withdrawn, reserved, shy, and prefers to do more with just the two of them. These kinds of issues would usually involve a compromise where neither is completely happy, but they have a goal both can live with.

9. <u>Creative Thinking</u>:

In our fast-moving world and society, it is easy for couples to pursue some different paths, which could complicate growing together. A common example is the executive husband who has a challenging, yet dynamic job, travels a lot, makes big decisions, has people reporting to him, earns a high salary, and gets a lot of management accolades. His wife is a stay-at-home Mom, raising three children, doesn't get out much, does all the housework and helps kids with their homework, drives them to every obligation, and has a domestic focus.

The trick for any couple that has different directions or focus to deal with is to share at great length with your spouse. Not only the facts of the differences but the emotional stresses or pleasures of their separate pursuits need to be shared. If a couple is totally separate each day, then a daily sharing or 'catching-up' is in order. Each needs to know and understand the positives and stresses of the other spouse's day. It also helps if the couple does some sharing of activities together such as joining a book club, a church, attending lectures, going to concerts together, and, in general, having a number of activities with your spouse. Both should attend as many of their children's activities as possible and discuss together any children issues.

10. Care and Maintenance of Your Marriage:

I once gave a series of lectures on marital maintenance, comparing it to the maintenance needed by any automobile or major piece of equipment. Marriage maintenance takes a lot of attention, planning and work. It doesn't just happen! Your car needs care and attention on a regular basis, as does a marriage. A car can't run without gas and a marriage can't run without love. Cars need oil to run smoothly; the marriage oil is communication. If something breaks on a car, you fix it... you don't just hope it will somehow go away. Cars require a 'checkup' to see if all is okay or if something should be changed or added. Marriage also needs regular checkup to see if something needs work or attention of some other kind. Men especially take care of their car; they wash it, clean it out, wax it, park it in the garage, especially in the winter, and look after it. It is the same with your marriage. You must give it attention, take care of it, look it over carefully and treat it with respect. Remember that in our car we are in control. We make it go fast or slower, turn corners, stop and go; in other similar ways, we control our marriage. Marriages don't guarantee happiness; we control their destiny and need to work to keep them strong and loving.

As we are driving our car, we may hear a rattle or strange noise, something we have not heard before. We don't just hope it goes away, we check it out. If it's too difficult, we go to a mechanic. Same with marriage, if it develops a squeak or a rattle, we need to check it out. Try hard to identify and fix the problem; and, if necessary, go to a marriage 'mechanic' which would be a therapist.

Cars have a purpose; they get you to where you are going in a hurry and in comfort. They are multi-functional so you can listen to music, the radio, talk together, be quiet; you are in control. Marriages are also multi-functional. It should have love, sharing, and mutual goals, meet each others needs, coordinate, plan and enjoy. Just like cars get you where you want to go, so should your marriage. As you travel in a car your trip has to be coordinated. It can't drive south or north at the same time... it's one or the other. If you want your marriage to work, in spite of some limitations, and if you feel you are in a loving relationship, the chances of picking the right direction are good.

Marriages need work, they need maintenance, as a good marriage isn't just good luck, it's hard work. Where you are going has to be coordinated with an agreed upon plan. Trips have to be planned together with how to get there being discussed. It is a together thing just like a marriage should be. Just as your work at your job or career, just as you maintain your car, just as you plan your day you need to plan and work at your marriage. Don't just assume you can drive forever without gas, or love, or never worry about an oil change or communication.

In summary, as has been mentioned previously, discussions should not have win/lose components. Not every problem is a 10; most are 1 or 2, and they should not be saved up. Attack problems with a goal of problem solving and be open-minded in the discussion. This includes facial expression and voice. If you smile and say, "Why did you do that?" in a calm voice you get better results than a frown and a raised voice saying "Why did you DO that?" If our goals are coordinated, positive and fulfilling, our behavior usually follows suit. Don't always focus on problem issues in your marriage. Try to promote and capitalize on its strength and fulfillment. If you focus on the positive, it will help you be more patient with the negative. Again have 'marital review' or 'life-style review' talks every now and then. From those talks, pick things you went to work on which will benefit you, your spouse, and the relationship. Keep track of your progress on those areas you want to improve. Tell your spouse often that you love them and that you love being married to them. That helps build up a more solid base for handling things that might arise. If your spouse doesn't reciprocate (and sometimes we men are not good at this!), say in a sincere way "Do you love me?" and if the answer is hesitant, it is time for a serious talk.

Marriages go through stages just as we all do in life. The early freedom of a new marriage often moves into the joy and stress of parenting. Parenting moves into more serious career issues, children's college and their expenses, and middle age issues may include health, health of our own parents and others. The later stages, (such as mine at this point), include retirement, financial concerns, the possibility of giving or receiving medical assistance, and time for the demands of grandchildren, all of which can be helped by being in a loving and supportive relationship.

No marriage is perfect as people can say or do hurtful things. Even persons who love their spouse and love their marriage can do hurtful things. Sometimes those things are misunderstood or misperceived by the other or not explained properly by the initial person. When a hurtful thing happens, the one who is hurt should not respond instantly (count to 10), think about what just happened or was said to make sure you saw it correctly. Do an inner check to see if you precipitated the problem by your behavior. Attempt to resolve the issue by saying "I felt really hurt when you said [___]." Hopefully there will be discussion followed by "I'm sorry" also followed by your understanding and forgiving your spouse if that is appropriate.

I have previously written about the need not to carry grudges, anger, or resentment around. I have used the example with couples of the pilgrim in John Bunyan's The Pilgrim's Progress carrying his bag of rocks over his shoulder. Don't do that! Forgive and Accept. I didn't say "Forgive and Forget" as that usually isn't the way it works. Forgive the spouse who has hurt or disappointed you and accept that they are not perfect, as you are not, and move on. Hopefully the benefits in your relationship will much outweigh those incidents where "Sorry and Forgiveness" are part of the solution.

◊

6
Changes in Relationship – Separation/Divorce

Change and loss in life are always difficult, even though the change may be desired or the loss anticipated. Even a mutually desired divorce has aspects of loss and for sure change. Loss of hopes and dreams, loss of the person you once wanted to be with, maybe loss of your home and possibly child care changes, which feel like a loss. The key in dealing with loss and change is to try not to focus on the loss but instead focus on new opportunities, new ventures, and a new and hopefully better life! Most of problem marriages are not 100% bad, and, in a separation or divorce some choose only to remember the few good times and try to forget the many bad ones. Or it could be the reverse, if they mostly want to get out of the marriage and remembering the problems helps them feel they made a good choice. Often facts vs. feelings come into play in many situations.

I have often seen couples where emotional or physical abuse is an issue. It is mostly husband to wife but not always. If the husband is abusive and the wife is physically and mentally hurt, then the husband apologizes, or convinces wife it was actually her fault, and then says he won't do it again. The wife believes him and also is afraid to leave, call the police, or file charges as change or leaving is very scary to her. She may also fear being alone, have financial issues, or is so insecure she believes it actually is her fault. So the process happens over and over and, in some cases, never stops. Fear of change is so strong that it overpowers a problem relationship, which is not a good decision.

Divorces are often seen as a failure of some kind; one or the other didn't work hard, did inappropriate things, or, in any case, didn't honor the marriage vows to be together "Until death do us part." I have seen many couples where a divorce is the most realistic solution. Love is gone, motivation gone, fear and hate abound, and no one wants to work at anything in the relationship. The complicated situation is if one of the couple feels all those negative things and the other is not sure or would like to try a little. They don't feel ready to leave and establish a separate home. That creates a very complex relationship problem. The therapy is to help each discuss their feelings/desires and together evaluate if anything can be changed or negotiated. This may take many weeks and involve lots of work, thinking, maybe changing on both sides. It is impossible to predict in advance where it will end, but I always work on the premise that if you learn to see the 'facts' more honestly, and understand reality more fully, feelings will often change or be modified. Seeing the facts more honestly also can mean that problems or issues are actually worse than one or the other thought.

Some couples have said they want to stay together "for the sake of the children." If that is the only reason, it often gives children the wrong idea of what is "marriage" or "family". They grow up seeing a cold and usually non-affectionate relationship. Even if the parents are cordial it is easy for children to sense problems. They may see an over abundance of anger, separate lives of parents and not a lot of loving family activities. It is my feeling that if a marriage is broken, and there are small children, it is better to have separate homes, where they can more easily see the 'best' of each parent.

In separation or divorce, it is better if there is no verbal or written spouse/parent bashing. I have seen many cases where each parent is blaming the other and trying to convince family/friends that they are the victim, the mistreated one, and the spouse is mean, cruel, and the bad one. It is better if the separated/divorced couple can at least have a casual friendship. This is most often difficult, especially at first when the emotional pain is the worst. If possible, a couple divorcing should have serious honest sharing with immediate family about what is to happen. If there is an attempt to understand why this is happening, and the effect of it on both, there may be the possibility of family acceptance, forgiveness and moving on. The couple may have anger and blame, including self-blame, which are difficult emotions to handle and need to be understood, hopefully reduced, so each can move on with the least amount of permanent scars.

Part of the task of dealing with any major personal event is to learn and gain something from the event. This takes thoughtful and honest reviews of the past and seeing how this has changed your life or modified your behavior. Often a recently divorced person will choose one of two paths, as they attempt to move on. One would be to feel desperate for a new relationship, as their self-confidence is gone, they feel unwanted and unloved, so they latch on to the first available potential partner. This is often done before they are really ready for that step. The other end of the scale is the person who is afraid to trust anyone they date. They may find fault very easily or feel afraid they will be hurt again, so they never commit, even if the new person is very worthwhile. Probably the best approach is to date casually, see different persons, and discover more who you are at this later stage and what kind of person you need in your life at this point.

A trial separation for a couple having problems can sometimes help lead to a final direction for them. The most important issue in couple separation is to be sure that each understands the purpose, goals, and rules of the separation. The purposes may be several but usually it is a kind of test case to see how it feels to be alone and to note how much, or little, the partner is missed. The goal is usually to help decide the future of the marriage and also time for either to work on personal issues that may have interfered in the marriage. The 'rules' are most difficult as it is a new situation for each, so there may be decisions to be made concerning many things. Some of them can be how often they see each other, do they have sex, can they date others, financial arrangements, and child visitation, or other decisions. Do they meet together for therapy, when do they have serious talks alone about how things are going, and how will they decide their next step.

Separations are challenging because the marital future is uncertain and most of us have the most difficulty with not knowing what is going to happen. If we know the end result of something, we may not like it but we face it because we know what it is and we learn how to deal with it. It is much harder to deal with uncertainty and most of us are not sure how to do that! Probably the worst use of a separation is if it goes 'on and on' with no discussion of progress or lack of it until one or the other just quits or files for divorce without it being part of a joint plan. Just drifting along is not making progress; it is just barely coping with what the situation is at the time. Don't drift into a decision. Instead, make a decision even though it is difficult. Once the decision is made it can be implemented, hopefully jointly, and both can begin the process of learning, accepting and moving on.

One never knows how a separation will affect the future of a relationship. I have seen situations where the couple really misses, needs, wants and wishes to be back with the partner. I have also seen just the opposite. In all cases, it is important to have a successful separation, so that it is a true test and judge of the quality of the relationship and the possibilities of a new start.

A divorce almost always stirs up strong emotions, and the emotions may differ for each person in a divorce situation. There may be some positive feelings of relief, joy, happiness, but much more common are feelings of loss, change, dreams gone, fear, uncertainty, blame, guilt or grief. Much has been written about the stages of grief and loss and the importance of dealing with those feelings and not denying them or pretending that they don't exist. The usual grief stages are most often identified as disbelief, doubt, bargaining, anger, grief and finally acceptance. Acceptance does not mean liking the end result but accepting it. In a divorce, the post-divorce goal is to accept the situation and learn more about yourself and what you want in a relationship. Work through the stages of grief/change and try to forgive yourself and former spouse for behavior and choices. Learn and move on. The past is over and a new and better future awaits you. Clean out and get rid of negative, blaming feelings and go forward with hope and new beginnings, gathering strength from your support system.

7
Addictions

Addictions are a common and difficult area with which to deal. The addict usually does not have an isolated problem, as frequently it impacts a spouse, siblings, possibly parents or children. You are not usually the only one impacted by your addiction. I realize there are exceptions, as homeless persons, those living on the street, or those in shelters often are alone, at least for that period of time. It is rare, but I have seen families where an addicted member, usually alcohol or drugs, has left and is missing and they have no idea where he or she is. By the time I have seen them they usually have given up hope of finding the addicted member.

Most cases of addiction are not that isolated, as addiction can take many paths. Alcohol, illegal drug abuse, prescription abuse, food, hoarding, sex, pornography, and gambling are probably the most common addictions. I have often seen persons with addictions who have what is called "addictive personalities". This means they may primarily be addicted to something like alcohol but also overdo medications, can't control eating habits, or are unable to set limits on their behavior in other ways. Probably the most common addictions I have seen are to alcohol or drugs, including prescription drugs. Most of them do not come in for therapy on their own, as they often don't want to or can't change their behavior. They come in because of family pressure or possibly a family intervention had recently occurred.

Current thinking suggests there may be a genetic base to many cases of addiction. Even if that is true in a situation, it doesn't solve the problem, or give the addict someone to blame. We 'are who we are' and we need to accept and deal with our own issues. Many addicts also suffer from another mental health issue, such as depression and anxiety. One of the papers I presented at a major conference was *Dealing With a Dual Diagnosis*. The concern about meds for someone with a dual diagnosis is the concern that there may be risk of addiction to the medication, which would make the problem worse. In past years, Alcoholics Anonymous groups often discouraged meds, but in recent years they have become more accepting.

I believe psychotherapy can help the addicted person, but I also believe psychotherapy and a 12-Step Program, such as AA, is the best treatment plan. Therapy will help you understand the problem, deal with the mental health piece of the problem, and help provide emotional strength to challenge and deal with the problem. AA and other 12-Step Programs provide ongoing support and a caring group to help the person in the recovery process.

Many addictions are of a black/white character. You don't just reduce or cut down your drug abuse, you stop it. Stopping a behavior takes insight, motivation, support and will power. The addicted person must learn to say NO... even though they would emotionally prefer another choice.

I feel attendance at a 12-Step Program, initially daily attendance, is very helpful and often necessary. I have heard many AA patients say to me, in a joking manner, "I switched my alcohol addiction to an AA addiction," for which I compliment them! The AA daily attendance, at least early in the recovery process, needs to be taken very seriously. It is also helpful to realize that the 12-Step program refers to their attendees as 'recovering', never, even after years of sobriety, as 'recovered'. It takes much emotional strength, encouragement and support to continue to say no, even when tempted. Therapy also helps the recovering addict to take pride and feel successful in their recovery process. It helps them to look at the benefits gained, relationships reviewed, control of life and destiny achieved, and to feel good about how their life has changed for the better.

In the recovering process, behaviors may have to change. If you give up the addiction, you need to redirect your actions to reflect that change; maybe exercise more, join an activity group, strengthen your spirituality and maybe attend your church more. Whatever your justification might have been for the addiction, you need to redirect those needs to worthwhile ventures and focus more outside of yourself and what you can do to make your life, your family, and your community better.

As I have said, there are many addictions in our society. Hoarding is not seen as often but can be a devastating addiction for the person and family. I have seen a number of those situations when the hoarder, usually pressured by family or friends, will come in to discuss their situation. Their motivation is usually not self-motivation but pressure from others. For the hoarder, the most common theme is that buying or collecting is an escape from tension, a comfort. The person may see it as fulfilling some unknown need, or "It gives purpose and direction to my life." Many hoarders choose that behavior after a serious emotional loss... a relationship, a spouse, job, and it helps them cope. Then they cannot stop. Some homes have been jammed for years; the addict allows no one in their home and every room becomes filled. Hoarding is common enough that the phrase "Find a Goat Trail" is a way of expressing how to move around in a room filled to the ceiling with 'stuff'. The most dangerous is the one who cannot throw away food or papers and after a time mice, rats or worse problems appear.

I love antiques and wrote an article for a weekly antique newspaper Antique Week, which was printed January 7, 2013. In the article I discussed the differences between collecting things for fun or a hobby and hoarding. At the end of the article, I wrote, "In summary, collections of things we love and appreciate can enhance our lives in many ways. We learn new things, enjoy the 'hunt', and love to touch and display our items for others to see. Most collectors have a personal or emotional attachment to their collections. It may be a family remembrance, maybe items that represent a current interest or something different that attracts your interest. That is not true for hoarders."

We do need to realize that hoarders should not be ridiculed, degraded, or misunderstood. Hoarding is an illness, much like serious depression or anxiety, and any of the other addictions. They need to be helped, not pitied or judged.

We also need to understand that hoarding is not a black and white situation. Not all persons with hoarding tendencies fill their homes to the top. The key is not to let that tendency get out-of-hand and to know when, where, and how to maintain control, enjoy our items and set limits on the number we purchase. The purpose is to enjoy them and share with pride our collections with others.

There are other mental health problems that border on addiction and include obsessive-compulsive traits such as bulimia, anorexia, the need to double-triple check everything, which is a compulsive behavior. For this chapter they are not considered 'addictions' but they do have some similar issues and problems.

Addictions are a serious problem and take serious effort when attempting to handle the disorder. Many alcoholics do not refer to themselves as addicts but rather problem drinkers or are in other kinds of denial. There is no clear definition of what makes something an addiction and some descriptions are vague. I recall a presentation on that area where the psychiatrist, with an addiction specialty, said, "Three or more drinks every day is one sign of an alcoholic." That is confusing because a 'drink' is not defined. Is a full glass of vodka a drink? Is one beer a drink? The usual definitions have to do with control, limits, and behavior. Is your drinking (or other addiction) within your control, can you set limits, does your drinking affect your behavior or your life? Effect upon family is also an issue and finances may enter the picture. Denial and rationalization are common attitudes.

One way to help the addict is to understand the purpose of the behavior. "The Bottle is My Friend" is an often-heard alcoholic comment. Is the addict totally stressed out, is he or she lonely or escaping some feeling by drinking, are they looking for comfort or a release from anxiety? If those emotional needs are present it will help the addict attempt to deal with those as well. In case of doubt about the severity of the problem, therapy would help, also some visits to a 12-Step Program such as AA, NA (Narcotics Anonymous), CA (Cocaine Anonymous) or similar would help would clarify the extent of the problem.

As I have mentioned, psychotherapy can help with addictions, but the most important issue is the strength to say "I quit!" and mean it. Family members need to be very supportive of recovering addicts and help them find a meaningful and productive life without their addictive behavior. This is often different for different addictions, as with gambling it might help to have some fun games or some other activities where you take fun chances to help counter the desire to gamble. Just remember... stopping a behavior, even though it may be destructive or hurtful, is difficult if that behavior feels necessary and important in a person's life.

Therapists always have stories to tell about success situations or failures. For me, I remember the situations that didn't work out well much more than the successes. I remember an older couple that came in for marital therapy. Most of the time I saw them together, but each did have at least one or two alone sessions with me. After about 6-8 sessions the wife came in alone, looking pained. I asked where her husband was and she said, "We buried him yesterday." Shocked, I asked what happened and found he had been drinking a lot one night, went to go up the stairs, and "his feet got ahead of him." He fell backward on the stairs, broke his neck and died. I asked about his drinking that night, and she said "Didn't he tell you he was an alcoholic?" Neither he, nor she, had ever discussed it, which made me feel badly for not checking out more completely whether or not this was a problem.

Another couple came in because the husband had gotten a substantial inheritance from the death of a parent, which was going to give the couple financial security for life. Six months after receiving the money, the wife discovered her husband had been secretly drinking and going to the casino, and all the money had been lost. You can imagine the anger and the guilt in a situation like that. She finally forgave him, but the marriage had a 'scar' that both had to overcome.

Another issue for addictions is that they are often progressive from bad to worse, especially, in the drug area, in which painkillers or other meds often need to be increased as the addict continues their use. Illegal drugs often have that same problem of increasing the usage to maintain the high. Even gamblers, who are losing, increase the bets to "strike it rich" and get back even with the outlay of their money. I live near Chicago, and almost every day there are shootings related to illicit drug use. Most shootings are between gang members who are also drug sellers protecting their territory. They have plenty of customers who make many purchases in spite of the dangerous territory and situation.

Another sad situation was a Nurse who came in for therapy because of depression and narcotic abuse. She had just been fired from her hospital job because she stole narcotics from patients on her unit for whom they had been prescribed. She was also in legal trouble and eventually lost her license. Judgment is often clouded when you are in desperate need of the substance of your addiction.

In summary, addictions can be terribly destructive to individuals and families. In the briefest words: Admit the problem, get help to give you strength to say NO, find support people or groups for your recovering process, find other activities or people to help you cope, and enjoy and progress on a new and different path in your future. If you are successful in these steps, you will move toward less longing for the thing you 'used' and hopefully enjoy to the fullest your new and improved life! I have seen it happen many times and it can be done!

◊

8
Lonely and Feeling Alone

Persons who find themselves alone, thinking nobody cares or likes them, feeling they are not included in things, or never sought out for friendship are often seen for therapy. One of the comments often heard early in therapy is, "Thank goodness, I have found someone who listens, understands and cares." My wife happened to notice I was writing about being lonely and alone and said, with a smile, that she had the following definition of loneliness: "Loneliness is when you are in a room with others and you sneeze, and no one says 'God bless you'." That might be one sign that feels real to some, but of course, I'm sure there are others! Loneliness is an emotion, but it may be based on interpretations of your world that are not accurate. People may feel that way in the middle of a crowd, sitting in church, or sometimes even at a family gathering. So why do some persons have those feelings? The following is a list of possible contributing factors:

- Basically insecure.
- Overly sensitive.
- Bullied or mistreated as a child.
- Hurt emotionally by others and now trusts no one.

- Personality-style being reserved, shy, quiet.
- Perceived failure in childhood or young adulthood, i.e. bad grades, social problems, physical inadequacies.
- Feeling different than others in areas such as health, appearance, race, religion, education, job.
- Not many social opportunities and what is available is not utilized.
- No siblings or minimum contact with existing siblings.
- In a school or work situation where they are often alone or isolated.

There are many opportunities for person-to-person relationships in almost all of society. Some people do live in isolated circumstances such as a country farm or even work in a foreign country where the language is difficult. Most of us have possible job, church, organization, neighbor, or community groups in which to participate, if desired. Lonely persons often do not take advantage of them because they don't want to 'risk' what might happen if they open themselves up for a sharing experience or relationship.

The first therapy step for a lonely or alone person is to discover why they don't want to or can't reach out to others and share. There are many people who are not heavily into the meeting, greeting, talking lifestyle and others who select friends more carefully and are not great socially but feel okay about it. They may be satisfied with their personality style, so it is not a problem. Those seeking therapy are unhappy about their situation and want help to change. As with many issues, you have to find an answer to the question… "What is really the problem here and what causes it?" There is almost no emotional problem with only one cause, but the major root causes for problem loneliness is insecurity, distrust, fear, suspicion, and in some cases, depression. Therapy can help identify issues and suggest areas to pursue, but the patient has to be willing to accept and confront the issues and begin to 'take risks'.

I have seen many situations where the person now understands the why of the problem, knows what to do that would help but is afraid to move out, take the risk and maybe end up being hurt or disappointed. As with most emotional problems… you have to try! Suffering in silence doesn't work! Taking a risk and stepping out is the only way to begin the process of change. Cognitive thinking also helps. If you realize that your perceptions of other people are incorrect, or maybe realize others don't actually think you are different and would like to know you better and incorporate you more into their lives, then these changed perceptions can change feelings. Seeing the actual 'reality' of who you are may also change your feelings about yourself. Therapy can help a person see and recognize good qualities and strengths. The more we feel good about ourselves, the more we will be able to be open and sharing with others.

It often doesn't take a major event or entirely new insight to help a person feel better about themselves. My 13-year-old granddaughter and a friend entered a Google contest at their school, and as part of it, made stickers for students with "beYOUtiful" printed on them. When they met someone in the hall, they were to say, "I am beautiful," which they all did.

The result was that the school had a great afternoon with lots of positive feelings expressed. A final comment from the two girls who organized and filmed the event, was: "Throughout the day, it was obvious that people felt a little bit more confident and proud to be themselves. We feel body and self-image are so important, especially at the age of a teenager. People do not realize their potential, but now we have realized that a small thing like our stickers and video can really help to change their world." Part of dealing with problems of any kind is to change what you can, work always on improvement, but accept what you must about yourself as no one is 100% happy.

Unfortunately, many people do feel lonely and without real friends. The saying, "feeling lonely in a crowd," does apply to many. It is difficult to have a full and meaningful life if you have only yourself to live with. Even a marriage may not solve that issue, as some feel lonely even with a partner, and some accept that at least they can share in the marriage better than in any other relationship. It is an issue that can be improved but needs ongoing attention and work, by the lonely one. As mentioned, some people are alone or feel lonely because of depression. A depressed person often lacks energy or initiative, doesn't see or want the benefits of being with others and prefers to be alone with their feeling of sadness and failure. If your personality choice is to not be socially active, to have only a few if any close friends and be alone a lot, that is fine (if you are content with that life-style.) If you are not content, and actually unhappy, reaching out in whatever way you can is essential to your own sense of feeling fulfilled and better able to cope with what has been your loneliness.

◊

9
Terminal Illness – Dying

All of us will face dying/death at some point in our lives and should put thought and preparation as we age and when dying becomes more of a reality. Examples of preparation could be signing and giving DNR orders to our medical physician and Power of Attorney for HealthCare to the one we choose. Discussions and wishes about death and dying should be held with spouse or other significant family. A booklet called *5 Wishes* has been helpful for many of the persons I have counseled who are older and doing long-range planning. But our main focus should always be on living a full and meaningful life until that time.

In the past few years I have volunteered to be a psychotherapist for some cancer groups and so have seen numerous patients dealing with cancer. Certainly not all were terminally ill, but many were, and I helped them the best I could to deal with the effects of their illness and to face dying and death with dignity. The adage, "You face death as you have faced life," is usually quite correct. People used to diversity and those who are survivors of life's challenges often face the end of life with better coping than those who have not faced challenges well. The task of dealing with a life-threatening illness, such as cancer is to face this difficult task and still 'have a life'! One cancer patient said to me, "I'm not going to let cancer define me," and she didn't! She lived with her cancer, died from it, but did not let it define how she lived or who she was during her illness.

I have discussed dying and related fears with many persons and there are some common themes. One is that most are not afraid to face death but are apprehensive about possible pain, dependency, and the process of dying. Dying is so individual that there are no guidelines to give people other than attitudes. Most people now have access to Hospice and Palliative Care which can be very helpful in the 'dying with dignity' process. I remember well a patient, who was a prominent musician, and had gone through months of chemo and radiation with diminishing success. His MD, a cancer specialist, finally said to him, "The cancer has beaten me; I am referring you to Hospice."

The patient reported that information in his next session with me and, during our talk he seemed to be somewhat detached. I asked him what he was thinking and he said, "I'm thinking about the second biggest event in my life." I asked him to explain and he said, "The first biggest was my birth and the second will be my death." Prior to his death, he and his wife explored, via the Internet, some unusual things to do that might cure him from the cancer. Most of them were very dubious, and the couple together decided quickly to focus on their enjoying, the best they could, the rest of their time together. They were able to do that, and they faced his death together with courage.

Facing death with dignity involves both practical and emotional issues. The practical are more obvious, including end of life care, an up-to-date will, preliminary funeral plans, and disposition of special 'things' that you want to give to family or others. The emotional is much more difficult to face. I have had patients who were afraid of the process of dying and would ask their MD, "How will I feel when I am dying?" MDs usually give general answers but try to deal with the patients' fears by explaining things that could be done to make that process less filled with fear or pain. A major emotional issue is to say good-bye to family and friends and to deal with any unfinished business existing with anyone. Things such as left-over anger or hurt from some past issues; blame for something you or they did; asking forgiveness or offering forgiveness to those who need it can be examples of ways to face their inevitable, being death. Also you can meet in person with everyone you can, to say good-bye. Keep in mind that this is very hard for them, as it is for you.

A woman I had seen for some time did the good-bye step with grace and dignity. When she was near death, I also shared a good-bye talk or two with her. She expressed to her husband how worried she was about him managing without her and her fears about her grandchildren being impacted by her death. At the end of that session, she said to me "I have one thing to ask of you." I, of course, wondered what it would be, and she said, "I want you to attend my funeral!" Of course I agreed and felt honored to do that, and did. This was another part of her planning and putting in place things for her death.
.

In the emotional sharing about dying it is common for persons to want to die after certain important events in their life have passed. Often things such as, "I want to see my son graduate from College," or, "I want to walk my daughter down the aisle at her wedding," are said. Sometimes events that have flexibility are moved up to accommodate the dying person's wish. Some persons have a list of things they want to do, or accomplish, before they are incapacitated or face death. Often called a Bucket List, it is usually a list of long hoped-for dreams. Having such a list of hoped for goals is fine as long as they are realistic and attainable. While working on the list, it is important to not only focus on what is left to do but also enjoy and feel good about those on the list which are already done.

Persons face death in many ways. My mother-in-law at age 96 was ready to die. Her health was failing, she was weak and barely able to function. She openly longed to see her husband and family in Heaven, which she felt would be her next home. She told my wife the songs she wanted sung at her funeral and asked me to write her obituary. I asked what she would like others to remember about her, and after a moment she said, "I want all my family and friends to know that I loved them."

In addition to this, she gave her family one of the best memories of a person saying good-bye. One day a few weeks before her death, she called my wife and asked if she would come to her home, as she felt that she was dying. That day my wife and our daughter went quickly to her bedside. She shared memories of her life and the treasures of their lives together. After much sharing, she asked them to reach about ten of her close family members on the phone so she could say good-bye. They were wonderful calls, sad but so deeply meaningful. She did not die until a few weeks later, but she knew her death was coming close, and she wanted to give statements of her love that day, in case it became too late.

I have seen many families torn apart prior to the death of a parent, especially if it is the last living parent. The children may quarrel about end-of-life issues with some ready to stop active treatment and others wanting to continue anything that may prolong life. It seems as if the latter is more often the case if the dying one is their mother. After death there may be arguments abut who gets what and anger at the person who was appointed executor. Quarrels may be over money available to each or fights over favorite items, especially jewelry or things that were important to the deceased parent. One family I saw was furious that someone else in the family had taken a small walnut end table that they had wanted. Both sides claimed it had been promised to them. Those kinds of problems make it clear that the person facing death should be very open about their wishes, both regarding their healthcare in the dying process but also for possessions and things that have family importance or value.

Many others in therapy have grief/guilt because of something they didn't do or didn't say to a deceased parent. I have encouraged many persons who have unfinished business with a loved one who has passed away, to write them a personal, thoughtful, intimate letter outlining their feeling in detail. Read it over a few times to make sure nothing was missed and then 'emotionally' mail it. Some persons have actually buried it at the gravesite; others put it away in a private safe place. In all cases, try to feel and accept that the parent has seen it and that you are forgiven. In my case, I had talked about death with my father, but he died more suddenly than expected, and I did not get to say a final good-bye, partially due to his living in another state. I wrote him a good-bye note, thanked him for being a good father, and told him I loved him and would miss him. I put it into an envelope and placed it in his open casket at the funeral. It helped me immeasurably to deal with the reality of his loss in my life.

Most persons facing death ponder their legacy for their children or family. Some want to leave a financial legacy, others maybe a business, and others possibly special valuable things. The most important, from my point of view, is to have your legacy be a life well lived and your children knowing they are much loved. Other legacies of that type might be stories of childhood, major incidents in your past that you want to record or family or ancestor history to pass on. I have encouraged patients to record, in a journal, feelings and history, which may be things that the children didn't really hear or know or especially about which they would never have thought to ask.

Attitudes about death can often be influenced by a person's religion, church affiliation or faith. (Those issues will be discussed more in the chapter on spirituality.) Persons with a strong faith background may feel that death is not an ending but rather an entrance into an eternal life in the hereafter. Others may fear they have not been good enough or strong enough in their faith, so they may be going to eternal damnation. Any dying person with issues related to their religion or faith should talk to an ordained clergyman, chaplain or specialist in the area of their doubt or concern.

Try to look at dying/death not as an option but an event you for sure will face some day. Prepare for it in a practical, legal way and try to say, to family and friends, whatever you want, and need to say. Then tell yourself you are now prepared, and that you do not need to worry about it or focus on it; instead you can live for today. The past is history, tomorrow is uncertain, but we do have today! It is also important not to become obsessed or overly dwell on the end of life issues and planning. Feel confident that you have planned well and then focus on living the best and most productive life that you can.

10
The Sandwich Generation

'Sandwich Generation' refers to those persons or couples who have adult children and also living older parents. A typical example would be a 45 year old who has 20-year-old children and 70-year-old parents. You are in the middle of those family members, with an age group above and below you – likened to a sandwich! At those ages, even grandparents may still be alive, and that would cause this young person to be in what's called the 'Club Sandwich Generation', with four generations of living relatives, all needing attention, and maybe some kind of care needs.

Part of the multi-generation problem is that at this point persons are living longer and handling serious illness better, which is great, but it does create more demands on the sandwich generation. Also an issue is that now many extended families do not live in close proximity, so care issues are complicated by distance. There also are cultural differences about caring for aging parents or grandparents that can complicate decision-making. The younger generations may not agree with or follow the same expectations as their parents did in the past.

The task of the center group is to no longer treat your children as little kids who need guidance and attention but to realize that they are adults, just like you. In our youth we don't like to think of our parents as dependent upon us, but as we all age that becomes a possibility. It is very difficult for an adult male to see his formerly high functioning father now forgetting things and not able to identify his granddaughter. I know, because that happened to me with my father. It was a very sad moment, but one that is a common part of the aging process.

Often feelings of family loyalty are challenged and tested. Examples include what you do if either parent or a child needs a money loan, or you have to decide whether you should visit your parent or child on your vacation. It is especially difficult if they are making requests or 'demands' on you. In the somewhat distant past in our country it was very common, and almost expected, that parents needing care and help would move in with one of their adult children. My paternal grandmother did that for a few years after my grandfather died, and it was a major family problem. She developed dementia and became very demanding. Finally, all the children gave up and she was placed in a nursing home. This solved the problem but gave everyone a sense of guilt.

Keep in mind that the parent who is cognitively intact but who has medical issues and cannot care for him/herself may become dependent on family. Parents who have always functioned well and independently now have to ask for help and are not happy about that. Fear of dependence on others is one of the major fear people growing old have to face. The problem is especially acute if the dependent parent has limited financial resources and cannot afford to move into a retirement community or nursing home. The tricky part of decisions for the sandwich group is to make decisions based on what is best for you and also best for the person in need. Too often emotionally made decisions are not good and not in your own best interests. You must look at your resources and needs as well as those of the needy family member. I have seen numerous families divided by an unpaid loan of several years ago or quarrel about the handling of parents' finances or their estates.

One of the most difficult decisions is often related to health and healthcare of parents. For many years, I was on the Ethics Committee of Lutheran General Hospital, and a common issue was a terminally ill parent who had not left any end-of-life requests or statements. Two children may have wanted mother to get all the care possible and two others wanting life support to be withdrawn, as to them mother was in pain and dying soon. Mother was comatose and could do or say nothing. These conflicts can be dramatic and damaging to relationships. I have also seen families quarrel about who should help a parent or grandparent, with resultant feelings that some siblings are not being fair and taking their share of the burden of care. There is often still a common stereotype that a daughter, not a son, should move the aging parent into their home or in other ways be the major caregiver. The daughter may feel her brother is avoiding responsibility or dumping tasks on her.

In summary, persons in the sandwich generation often have to make difficult decisions, which can be influenced by guilt, loyalty, love or other emotional or practical issues. The key is to recognize the emotional components but be guided by the reality of: "What does the parent in need really need? What is best for me, the child? What are the realistic things I can do to help my child, parent, or grand-parent?" Keep in mind emotional and supportive sharing should be available from you, but time and money should have realistic limitations. Sometimes family pressures can cause resentment and blame, which are emotions, but not facts. So don't let your emotions force you, or stop you, from doing what you can and should to help a significant family member.

I have told hundreds of patients to do what they can to help and care for family, but that their major job is to take care of themselves and their immediate family. When that is accomplished, then do what is reasonable to care and give to others or help them to find other resources to help them with their dependency or financial needs. There may be times when you need to say "No," or "I can't do it all," to the family member you love. There may be lots of love and caring but reality must also enter in to our extended family issues and decisions. We need to do what we can but not try to do what we can't!

11
Spirituality and Mental Health

Spirituality and Mental Health are two areas that can be very much related to each other but are difficult to define. Spirituality especially can mean different things to different people, partially depending upon your faith or religion. Even the Internet ends with a description of spirituality by saying "There is no single agreed upon definition of Spirituality." For the purposes of this chapter, I will think of spirituality as a belief in a "Higher Power," most often referred to as "God," to whom we look up to, believe in, pray to, and feel is a personage who can give us strength, guidance, and support. People have different levels of spirituality from casual acceptance to strong devotion to this Higher Power.

Many articles and books have been written about how our mind, body, soul and spirit are all connected. We are a product of many parts, including genetics, environment, family and belief systems. In times of crisis, mental health or other, we often turn to our resources for guidance, help and support. A major study done by a psychologist at Lutheran General Hospital, where I worked for so many years, studied what was most helpful for persons suffering from major or terminal illness and facing death. The study found that a family support system and a strong faith in God helped the most.

It is difficult to prove that spirituality can help our lives, but I have seen many patients whose faith has helped with many mental health problems in the following ways:
- Less hypertension
- Less stress – even during difficult times
- Less depression
- More positive feelings
- Greater psychological sense of wellbeing
- Better ability to look for purpose and meaning in the midst of trouble

Spirituality also cannot cure medical or psychological problems, although there are some who believe that it can, but certainly it is one source of help. Many spiritual persons attend a house of worship, and there they may get the support of worship leaders or other attendees, which provides a sense that they are not alone, and that can often help. Many patients have reported that feeling that there is a Higher Power that they can talk to, ask for help, be understood, and possibly receive guidance or enlightenment from is often powerful in its positive effects.

I am confident that a spiritual life, which includes belief, prayer, and trust in the higher power, can help us deal with our problems. The process of how spirituality can help can differ from person to person. Some obvious ones are the power of prayer, fellowship and support of people in the spiritual community, and trust that the Higher Power loves you, hears your prayers, and is giving you strength, direction and support.

Prayer is beneficial in more than one way. The person praying for help often verbalizes (mentally or vocally) their problems and often just identifying and admitting a problem is helpful. Feeling heard and understood by a Higher Power helps them to not feel alone and they may feel insight and clarity because of the prayer. Sharing problems with others in your house of worship or a clergyman can also help so you don't feel alone. Feeling someone else understands and cares, and wants to help can be inspiring.

It is helpful for the spiritual person to feel his/her spirituality will help them to be a more loving person and one reflecting spiritual values. Spiritual persons are not immune from life's problems. We can be depressed, anxious about things, worried, and have health or social pressures in our lives. Our spiritual values and beliefs should help us to better deal with those issues, to accept what we must, and make our lives as full of meaning as we can. A spiritual life well lived is not a problem free life but will help us deal with or accept problems with increased strength, support and a sense of peace. Spiritual values also include accepting, helping and loving others.

But the other side of spirituality is that, in some cases, it can cause doubt, stress, and uncertainty within the spiritual person, especially for those who feel they have a strong faith and a solid belief system. The following are some situations where spirituality may raise questions and doubts about the effectiveness of their belief system may occur.

1) Prayers appear to not be answered: This might occur related to a personal crisis, health issues, stress, anxiety, fear or a feeling of being overwhelmed and not knowing what to do. The fervent prayer is "God help me with this problem," but nothing appears to change and in fact may get worse. Additional prayers do not appear to change anything and there is a risk the spiritual person begins to have doubts or even anger directed toward God. Rather than saying that maybe God's answer to their prayer is not the answer they want, they may have the additional problem of feeling ignored by God and not helped at all.

2) Major illness, cancer, any long-term debilitating health issue: I have recently worked with many cancer patients as a volunteer for a cancer care organization. The issue of "Why me" has come up often, especially if the patient is younger, has family responsibilities, and has led a 'spiritual' life up to the point of their diagnosis. Why would God do this or allow this to happen is asked. Some go on to struggle with, "Am I being punished for something?" Prayers to be cured are not answered in the way they would like and their trust in God might be weakened. Persons who have a different prayer such as "God help me cope with this problem, give me strength to do my best, help me learn from this trauma and be a better person," are using their spirituality in a more positive way.

3) Am I doing enough: Some persons are very self-critical and see their problems, shortcomings and faults as signs they are not spiritual enough. They feel inadequate, as if they are failures, and not good examples of a spiritual person. If they are already feeling insecure about their life's situation, this could make them feel even worse. It might become one more thing over which to be depressed or anxious. They look at their behavior rather than their attitude. No one is perfect, but we can still love God, feel loved by Him and do the best we can.

4) Jealousy: Spiritual persons can have difficulty understanding why the atheist living next to them has a great job, makes lots of money, is seemingly happy, yet never goes to church or any house of worship. In fact he/she may make fun of spiritual things and be proud of their lack of belief. The spiritual person could ponder the issue of, "Is God Unfair? Why doesn't He reward me and punish unbelievers?" They can forget that spirituality is not how much you own, or how famous you are, but who you are and what you believe inside your heart, mind and soul.

5) Catastrophic personal events: A spiritual person may fear losing his/her job, maybe being demoted, so prays for God's help and next day actually loses the job. "WHY!" is often asked, "I did my best, and prayed about it, so why didn't God do something?" After a car accident... "Why didn't God intervene, so this wouldn't happen to me?"

6) World problems: Spiritual persons may wonder why God allows plane crashes, ISIS killings, and mass murders all over the world! If God is Love, why doesn't He do more to save us and stop all this senseless murder, rape, crime we read about every day? I live near the city of Chicago, which has had many murders in the last few years. I have heard comments like, "Why does God let this all

happen?" The spiritual person may struggle with the issues of behavior and control over life's events vs. feelings, emotions, love and who we really are. To accept the unacceptable and to love others, good or bad, is part of the spiritual message that gives us strength to face all of life's challenges and to accept life as it is, not how we would like it to be.

In summary, a spiritual person does have their beliefs to help deal with health or mental health issues... not necessarily to totally solve them, but to assist with attitudes, faith, support and guidance. Much of that approach is similar to psychotherapy. Understanding yourself better, developing good self-esteem, feeling more confident, becoming emotionally strong and developing a good support system are all things that spirituality and psychotherapy work together to accomplish.

12
Growing Old With Grace and Dignity

Of all the chapters in my book, this one is the most currently realistic for me. I am 85 and usually that is considered 'old'. However many of my friends define old as five years older than whatever their current age is! I am going with that definition!

We are all in the process of aging, even if we are young at this time. It is hard to define what old age really is, as much of 'old age' is influenced by our attitudes toward life. Usual definitions include actual age, retirement, maybe getting Social Security or Medicare, or having moved to a smaller home or a retirement community. For our purposes in this chapter, we will think of being older as the next stage in our life… including things like not being employed fulltime, having older children, slowing down a bit, possibly parents gone and a changed and probably modified lifestyle.

Facing growing old is something we all should begin to prepare for in our mid years or earlier. There are well-known practical things like financial planning, completing a will, deciding on our end-of-life issues and handling any inheritance questions, which are the ones we usually think of first.

There are some common changes relative to growing older that I have seen often in working with near retirement or older persons. One issue is the overly anticipated stage of retirement, not being employed fulltime, able to relax all day, play anytime, and maybe move to a warmer climate… fun, fun, fun! They so look forward to the future that they don't enjoy their life's journey as they should. Their goal is so much 'down the road' focused that they lose track of the meaning of today.

Many end up finding that the older stage is not really what they thought it would be and become depressed, discouraged and feel they have lost purpose and direction in their lives.

A second group is those who are overwhelmed by and unprepared for the many changes that occur as one enters the growing old stage. They are faced with lower energy levels, nothing constructive to do, have aches and pains, no new friends, old friends are moving and dying, and they feel unimportant. They may find a fulfilling career hard to give up and all the changes required in aging difficult to face and hard to accept.

The following are several areas to look at that I have discussed with persons growing older and trying to adjust to that process. The major reason to consider them is to help find direction, purpose, goals, enjoyment and accomplishment in the stage of older age.

1) Have a realistic attitude when you think and plan for aging. Make that stage feel like another opportunity in life. Obviously, some changes and new directions have to be made, but look forward to them as new opportunities for growth and accomplishment. I have had many older patients who say things like, "For me, the Golden Years are not golden!" Try to anticipate changes and look forward to them. Enjoy the journey as you prepare for the stage of old age.

2) A healthy lifestyle is important as we age and should include weight control, routine MD check-ups, nutritious diet and especially activities and exercise. Growing old is not a time to stop taking care of oneself. Actually, giving attention to the physical health aspect can play a big role in successfully handling aging. Keep track of any physical issues such as balance problems, difficulty climbing stairs or walking, or hearing and vision loss.

3) Persons who have had a career that they love and active lifestyle with lots of travel and adventure may find aging more of a challenge than others. One of the important tasks of growing older is to establish new, possibly more realistic goals, for your age group. Plans, hopes, dreams and a positive attitude are essential for a fulfilling old age. Try not to grieve what you have lost, but anticipate new opportunities.

The following is a specific list of activities, plans, and challenges that I have seen many older persons select and use to make their stage of life more fulfilling and meaningful:
- Never stop learning or growing.
- Engage in an active social life.
- Have a realistic, challenging and fun Bucket List.
- Cultivate new interests and activities.
- Join appropriate groups… maybe a senior center, church, library or fitness center.
- Volunteer at a local place of interest, charity, hospital or not-for-profit endeavor.
- Attempt to face and accept the reality of aging, especially to the slowing-down process.
- If Spirituality is an interest, be sure to cultivate and strengthen it as a source of support as needed or wanted.

- Be as active as you can! Don't play the 'old age card' to get out of doing what you could/should be doing.
- Enjoy what you have; don't grieve over past pleasures or what you used to be and do.
- Memories of the past – the good old days – are nice to remember, but your task is to make more memories now that have meaning and that you can enjoy at this point in time.

Many older persons have discussed the importance of music both as a memory and as an opportunity. A large number of retirement communities now have remembrance or reminiscence groups, where memories of old music favorites are discussed after playing the songs. If related music interests, such as singing or dancing, have been a part of a person's life, they should be continued for as long as physically possible. It's great to listen to the old songs, but there are a lot of new songs available too.

Sharing your background, childhood memories and maybe cultural issues can be meaningful to your children and especially grandchildren. Show them old photos, talk about your parents and grandparents with them, and share your past highlights or past struggles. Let them really get to know who you are! A special note, to be opened when you are gone, written to children or special friends, telling them how much they meant to you and how much you loved them, is a very meaningful legacy gift.

There are many other activities, duties, expectations that persons who are aging should face. Some of these are the previously mentioned practical ones of wills, trusts, and the disposition of things. These can become an emotional struggle if there are several dependents or if there are stepchildren as part of the process. One person I know had many things and many relatives, so she took pictures of almost every single item of importance and wrote on the back the name of her chosen recipient. She also wrote a description on the back of the items with any known history, of the item including its age.

The aging process does not mean you stop living! Keep as active as you can, cultivate friendships, plan new activities, be as adventurous as you are able, and learn things new and different.

Some older persons look ahead with much fear and anticipation: "How much time do I have left?" "Will I become dependent and need care?" "Do I have enough money saved up?" are common questions. The goal of any looking forward at length should not be to predict when things might happen but to prepare in the best way you can and try not to worry about things beyond your control. Work at solving problems or issues which you can control and don't focus on the ones over which you have no control.

In summary, the aging process is something we cannot avoid, but we can control attitudes and behaviors about it. There are things we can do to make the most of it. Having plans and goals is important in any stage. So is the process of helping others and making a difference in other people's lives as we can. Developing resources for support are essential. Spend time with family and friends, as their support and encouragement will be of utmost importance. Use spiritual resources to give you courage and strength and use your 'bucket list' as a challenge and as a sense of accomplishment that will bring pride when you cross out each item. Make memories, enjoy what you can and accept what you cannot do. Plan as you can for your future and look forward to it. As it says in the old song *The Gambler*, "Know when to hold 'em, know when to fold 'em, know when to walk away and know when to run."

13
Finding Meaning, Purpose and Direction in Life

This is a very important area and challenging, as individuals have very different hopes, dreams and goals that reflect their purpose and meaning for their lives. If your meaning and purpose is to be rich and buy lots of things, then your goal is to 'Make Money'. If your meaning and purpose is to serve your God and minister to others, you could become a priest, a clergyman or a very active church member and/or volunteer to help carry out the mission of your church.

The point is we have different hopes and goals, partly reflecting our family values and persons who have influenced us in our growing up years. Many persons come to therapy because they have no direction in their lives, not much gives them pleasure or fulfillment, and all they want to do is somehow earn enough to live and then live in seclusion, wanting to be alone. In some cases, goals are influenced by a mental health issue, such as depression and may also be affected by low self esteem, lack of confidence, past failures, lack of support or inadequate preparation for their chosen goal. No one should ever rate hopes and goals as good/bad, as they are very personal and selected by you.

Here are a few guidelines to consider which might help in this area. Make sure your goals are your personal goals, not pushed into you by parents or someone else. They should reflect what you wish to achieve and will help you feel you are accomplishing whatever you have chosen. Also be as clear as you can in your thought process about what your goals will be. Freud is reported to have said, "Be careful what you wish for; you might get it!" The point here is that wishes are not facts and not understanding what you really want can be devastating. Most goals take time: If you want to be a doctor, it will take years of study; if you want to be ditch-digger, you can do it much more quickly!

The point is that we should all put much thought into our purpose and direction in life and understand what makes us feel happy and fulfilled. We also have to try to proceed. It is easy to dream, think, and plan, but action is required at some point. There are goals that follow a more natural course of living and some are more far reaching. To finish high school, get married, have a couple of children, work at the same job (whatever it is) for 40 years, retire, move into a retirement community and finish life is a standard goal for many. All are important goals but others want a major degree, a profession, money, a collection of fine art, trips to the symphony, investments and to retire in style. We need to do what fulfills us and does not affect negatively our families and significant others. The search for happiness is not easy, and we must do something about it; doing nothing is not doing something! At a minimum, our goals should be well thought out, attainable in time, open to change and adjustment if necessary, and helpful to our sense of achievement and accomplishment.

Most of the well-adjusted persons coming in for mental health help, such as depression, are persons who have a balanced group of goals for their life. Some may be a little more important, but all help them feel good and mark their identity. They usually have purposes and goals that make them feel fulfilled but also are of help to others within family or community. Goals can certainly be personal such as trying to obtain money or things but also can be extensions of your interest in your belief system. Being active in your church, supporting mental health agencies, serving on your school board, volunteering, giving money – all are ways to help others but also avenues to making yourself feel good.

Finding meaning and purpose in life is clearly helped by having realistic hopes, dreams, goals and positive actions. There are other things we can do to find meaning and purpose and several have been mentioned in previous chapters but are summarized here:

1) If you have problems, identify them and ask for help and support from family, friends, and professionals if necessary.

2) Don't be embarrassed or try to hide your individual problems. Friends can be very supportive and understanding when we honestly share.

3) Utilize or seek-out spiritual resources which could include a house of worship, prayer group, or men's or women's group that shares your interests.

4) If you pray, trust God to answer and try to accept and understand what the answer seems to be. Maybe it's No or Not Now!

5) Use meditation and quiet times. Turn off your worries and focus on your inner self. Give yourself a half-hour break or so frequently.

6) Take action; don't sit and wait for a miracle.

7) Use your cognitive skills to analyze your situation. Feelings are not necessarily facts! Do I truly understand my problems and their possible solutions?

8) Remember you are not alone if you are having trouble with mental health issues or in finding meaning and purpose in life. (Research has shown that over 20% of us have a diagnosable mental health problem!) Realize that others have suffered the same problems, so search out trusted friends and share and learn.

9) Look outside yourself and your own issues and help others. Donate, volunteer, and help out those in need. Find a cause and support it. Help out at a soup kitchen, a woman's or homeless shelter. Doing for others often helps us keep our problems in perspective and may help us feel more fulfilled, purposeful and in moving in the direction that we desire for ourselves.

In summary, the most fulfilled people I know do have drives to accomplish things that benefit themselves and also their spouse or other family members and their community. A broad group of goals is better and certainly some may have higher priority. Include others in your goals, including others outside your family. Work towards goal attainment but enjoy the work and feel satisfied with what you have done. We all need purpose and direction in our lives. The task is to clarify what form these take, and that they are realistic and attainable. One important part of goals towards purpose in life is to not focus entirely on the final goal or the major purpose to the exclusion of the journey. Life is for living, not only to search for what you don't have or want to get, but enjoying the moment. Remember the adage, "Yesterday is history, tomorrow is uncertain, but we do have today."

A beautiful narrative, which I have given to many couples, is by Robert Hastings and is entitled *The Station*. It has and continues to have a lot of meaning to me, and I hope to those of you who read it.

THE STATION by Robert J. Hastings

Tucked away in our subconscious is any idyllic vision. We see ourselves on a long trip that spans the continent. We are traveling by train. Out the windows we drink in the passing scene of cars on nearby highways, of children waving at a crossing, of cattle grazing on a distant hillside, of smoke pouring from a power plant, of row upon row of corn and wheat, of flatlands and valleys, of mountains and rolling hillsides, of city skylines and village halls.

But uppermost in our minds is the final destination. On a certain day, at a certain hour, we will pull into the station. Bands will be playing and flags waving. Once we get there, so many wonderful dreams will come true and the pieces of our lives will fit together like a completed jigsaw puzzle. How restlessly we pace the aisles, damning the minutes for loitering... waiting, waiting, waiting for the station.

When we reach the station, that will be it! we cry. "When I'm 18." "When I buy a new 450SL Mercedes Benz!" "When I put the last kid through college." "When I have paid off the mortgage!" "When I get a promotion." "When I reach the age of retirement, I shall live happily ever after!"

Sooner or later we must realize there is no station, no one place to arrive at once and for all. The true joy of life is the trip. The station is only a dream. It constantly outdistances us.

"Relish the moment" is a good motto, especially when coupled with Psalm 118:24: "This is the day

which the Lord hath made; we will rejoice and be glad in it." It isn't the burdens of today that drive men mad. It is the regrets over yesterday and the fear of tomorrow. Regret and fear are twin thieves who rob us of today.

So, stop pacing the aisles and counting the miles. Instead, climb the mountains, eat more ice cream, go barefoot more often, swim more rivers, watch more sunsets, laugh more, and cry less. Life must be lived as we go along. The station will come soon enough.

64652464R00092

Made in the USA
Lexington, KY
15 June 2017